A PLUME BOOK

WHAT THE FUN?!

© Maria Ponce

Media personality and parenting expert Donna Bozzo has appeared on TV shows and television stations across the country, including *Today*, ABC7 Chicago, *Great Day Saint Louis*, Veria Living TV, NBC5 Chicago, WGN-TV, *You & Me*, *Good Day Chicago*, *Daytime*, *Good Morning Arizona*, CBS2 Chicago, and *The Morning Blend*. Donna worked for many years as a reporter, TV producer, writer, and creative director, and has written for *Family Circle*, *Brides*, *Working Mother*, *American Baby*, *Chicago Parent*, *Make It Better*, *Chicago Tribune*, and *Going Places*. Donna has a journalism degree from Indiana University and lives in Winnetka, Illinois, with her husband and three daughters.

What the
FUN?!

~~~~~~~~~~

427 Simple Ways
to Have Fantastic
Family Fun

~~~~~~~~~~

Donna Bozzo

A PLUME BOOK

PLUME
An imprint of Penguin Random House LLC
375 Hudson Street
New York, New York 10014

Copyright © 2016 by Donna Bozzo
Penguin supports copyright. Copyright fuels creativity, encourages diverse voices,
promotes free speech, and creates a vibrant culture. Thank you for buying an
authorized edition of this book and for complying with copyright laws by not
reproducing, scanning, or distributing any part of it in any form without
permission. You are supporting writers and allowing Penguin to continue to
publish books for every reader.

 REGISTERED TRADEMARK—MARCA REGISTRADA

LIBRARY OF CONGRESS CATALOGING-IN-PUBLICATION DATA
Names: Bozzo, Donna, author.
Title: What the fun?! : 427 simple ways to have fantastic family fun / Donna
Bozzo.
Description: New York, NY : Plume, [2016]
Identifiers: LCCN 2015049252 (print) | LCCN 2016005129 (ebook) |
ISBN 9780399185519 (paperback) | ISBN 9780399185526 (ebook)
Subjects: LCSH: Family recreation. | Amusements. | BISAC: FAMILY &
RELATIONSHIPS / General. | FAMILY & RELATIONSHIPS / Parenting /
General. | FAMILY & RELATIONSHIPS / Education.
Classification: LCC GV182.8 .B695 2016 (print) | LCC GV182.8 (ebook) |
DDC 790.1/91—dc23
LC record available at http://lccn.loc.gov/2015049252

Printed in the United States of America
10 9 8 7 6 5 4 3 2 1

All photos courtesy of Donna Bozzo.

DEDICATED TO:

My husband, Matt
You make all my dreams come true.

My daughters, Juliana, Grace, and Ava Francesca
You put the fun in family.

My sister, Jen
Dandelions and bike parades. It all started with you!

And to my other "sister," Shannon
Without my Thelma, this book would not be possible.

CONTENTS

Section One

Section Two

Miss Lucy had a baby
His name was Tiny Tim
She put him in the bathtub
To see if he could swim.

He drank up all the water
He gobbled up the soap
He tried to eat the bathtub
But it wouldn't go down his throat.

Miss Lucy called the doctor
Miss Lucy called the nurse
Miss Lucy called the lady with the alligator purse.

In walked the doctor
In walked the nurse
In walked the lady with the alligator purse.

"Mumps," said the doctor
"Measles," said the nurse
"Nonsense," said the lady with the alligator purse.

"Penicillin," said the doctor
"Castor oil," said the nurse
"Pizza!" said the lady with the alligator purse.

Out walked the doctor
Out walked the nurse
Out walked the lady with the alligator purse.

Here's to silly, fantastic wisdom!

—Donna Bozzo, aka the Lady with the
Alligator Purse

Section One

~~~~~~~~~~~

They who dance are thought mad by those who hear not the music.

—OLD PROVERB

CHAPTER ONE

What the Fun?!

*The most important thing is to enjoy your life—to be happy—
it's all that matters.*

—AUDREY HEPBURN

Where is the fun in your family's life?

You know, the F-U-N?

Are you trying to figure out where it went? Is it trampled
by should-haves and would-haves and if-I-could-haves, worries,
mental juries, and frazzled scurryings-about? Is it buried under endless routines or lost in a long line of boring carpools?

Then this book is for you.

It is so easy to lose our foothold in fun. Keeping up with
this crazy game of family life gobbles up our days and takes a
tasty chunk of our nights. *Time* magazine is now calling parenting America's most competitive adult sport as we drown in
endless kid athletic schedules, music lessons, and enrichment
activities. We are stressed, we are tired, and somehow in the
tornado of our crazy, jumbled days we are still *bored*. We've
sunk so deep in the day-to-day crunch of life we've forgotten
how to make things fun. And we've forgotten (or maybe we

never knew) how important it is for us to enjoy our days together. Day by day, we are missing out on the true prescription
for a good life—FUN.

> *Happiness must be grown in one's own garden.*
>
> —MARY ENGELBREIT

Want proof? Just look to the science of fun. Creating more
fun in your life makes you happier, makes you healthier, and
helps you live longer. Researchers, philosophers, physicians,
and social reformers have spent lots of time finding out what
we still know today: *fun is good for you.* Sigmund Freud pio-
neered many studies proving that fun helps us connect and
wards off fear, anger, anxiety, and other undesirable emotions.
And other studies followed—the biggest tracking the lives of
180 Notre Dame nuns for five decades. It turns out the happier nuns—nuns described as focusing on joy—lived as much
as ten years longer. Bingo!

> *Never, ever underestimate the importance of having fun.*
>
> —RANDY PAUSCH, *THE LAST LECTURE*

Take Your Medicine

Creating more fun in your days is good for your health.
Dutch sociologists found that happiness protects against ill-
ness, with the most satisfied people gaining almost an extra
ten years of life—almost as powerful a measure as quitting

smoking by age thirty-five. And creating fun and happiness in your life has absolutely no side effects. What's more, fun is fantastic for your kids. According to *Psychology Today*, creating a happy childhood for your children—defined as doing things as a family and creating fun traditions—gives kids greater social connectedness and an enhanced sense of self and healthy behaviors. Plus, get this: *not having fun* is actually bad for them. Researchers who studied New Guinean cultures found that children suffer serious consequences when they are raised by parents who devalue fun. And in a forty-two-year study, a Baylor University researcher found that kids who don't have fun childhoods don't grow into happy, well-adjusted adults. He interviewed twenty-six convicted murderers and found they all had one thing in common: *they never played as kids.* Even the National Institute for Play found that play-deprived children and adults have greater communication problems and more intense conflicts with people overall.

Depression in teens is on a swift rise, *and* get this—it's attributed to a decline in play in childhood, according to research just released by San Diego State University. Even schools are taking note. A west Philadelphia high school recently created a fun class. The goal? To teach fourteen- and fifteen-year-olds how to *own* their happiness by learning how to create fun in their lives in the hope that this important life skill will follow them into adulthood. Can you imagine how much influence you will have on your children by modeling fun at home?

Children need models more than they need critics.

—JOSEPH JOUBERT

///

! FUN FACT:

Scientific studies performed at McGill University found that baby rats that are fondled and licked by mothers generally handle stress better than rats whose mothers don't. And this is telling: if you switch the rats and put the stressed rats with the physically affectionate mothers and the happy rats with nonaffectionate mothers, they will begin to reverse.

\\\

Putting more fun in your days not only makes your children happier—it will make your great-grandchildren happier as well. After twenty-five years of studies, German scientists found that when parents become happier (or unhappier), so do their children. They found that the link between happy parents and happy kids can stretch for generations to come. Why is this? It's because we organically pass our values and behaviors on to our kids.

If you make fun a priority in your life—by focusing on family values, social connections, work-leisure balance, community participation, and regular exercise—*your kids will do the same.* Scientists even found a lifelong happiness dividend (or unhappiness dividend) due to parenting long after the children have left home. Plus, they found all this happiness has a reciprocal effect. Happy kids = happy parents through the years, because families continue to pattern each other for life. Happy-happy.

Creating fun in your family's life also has immediate advantages for your children.

By focusing on folding fun into your family's life, you will make your children *players* in life. And you will help them de-

! FUN FACT:

According to the American Academy of Pediatrics children's playtime has been reduced at home over the last few decades because of today's hectic lifestyles, leaving kids with higher levels of stress, anxiety, and depression.

velop resiliency. Both a Sesame Workshop study and a large study by the American Psychological Association found that when children feel their parents *enjoy* them and *play* with them, it helps them build a resilient brain architecture. Resilient children (and adults) cope better with stress and change. A playful attitude helps us all weather the storms of life better.

One-and-Done Fun

Fun Things You Should Try at Least Once

SLEEP IN A BACKYARD TENT AS A FAMILY
You don't have to wander far for a night under the stars.

WATCH THE SUNRISE TOGETHER
Every day's beginning is a gift!

HAVE DINNER *UNDER* THE DINING ROOM TABLE
Yep, yep, yep—place mats, plates, cups, and spoons. Set the table down under.

START A HOBBY TOGETHER
It doesn't matter what you do, as long as you do it together.

HAVE BREAKFAST AT THE PARK
For us, it's bagels on the beach!

HAVE A PAJAMA DAY
Spend the day together and all stay in your jams relaxing, playing, reading, and watching movies.

You get to decide what the tenor of your life will be. You can decide the flavor of your family life. So why not make it fun? Decide right now—right this very second—that you are going to carve out good times and happiness for you and your family. And why not? I mean, when you look back at your life, do you ever wish you could cut out the fun times? All those fantastically silly times? Would you take back one? I wouldn't— not a single silly, giggly, *can-you-believe-this-is-happening* good time. If I had to guess, I bet you wouldn't either.

Happiness . . . not in another place, but this place—not for another hour, but this hour.

—WALT WHITMAN

Sure, we all have some tough tumbles—that's the ticket price for sticking around the ol' revolving Earth for a few spins—but try to stop yourself from making good times hard. Don't rob yourself of fleeting sunshine. Make fun a priority in your own life, squeeze it into bits of days, every day—and your children will follow in your footsteps. They will grow up to be adults who have learned *how to enjoy life*. What more could you want for your children and yourself?

Yes. Yes. Yes. I know. I know. Who has time for fun? We are not all sitting on our rumps all day every day. It would all be so flippin' easy to power-fold fantastic fun into our lives if we weren't all so—duh—*busy*. I get it.

Okay then, want to know the secret? Here you go: the key to fun is to make it peasy, peasy, turn-around easy. This book will show you how.

It's either easy or impossible.   —Salvador Dalí

CHAPTER TWO

Getting Started

It is fun to have fun but you have to know how.

—DR. SEUSS

So you're convinced. Now what? Call in the clowns, confetti, and mechanical monkeys? Hit the trapeze? Dance 'til dawn? Fly to France?

Well, not exactly.

The fantastic thing about fun is it comes in a trillion flavors. What is fun to you? As simple as it sounds, do you *really* know? What seems fun to everyone else may not be necessarily fun to you. Oftentimes, when it comes to fun, we just go with the flow. We do what everyone else is doing. We spend too much time doing the types of things that *seem* like they *should* be fun, but they are not crazy-fun *to us*. We get married, start families, and try our best to fold into the community around us—work, our neighborhoods, church. We become what I call Fun Zombies, just treading along doing what everybody else tells us we *should* be doing. And by doing so, we inch by inch begin to rob ourselves of the good life. Did you join a tennis club only to slowly learn that your family hates to play tennis? Do you see the same family friends for dinner again and again—and find everyone in your family complaining that they had nothing to say to your guests? Did a family cruise seem like a good idea, except your family loves to explore destinations on a whim with no time limits? Do you have a shelf full of board games nobody plays?

First, Figure Out Your Unique Fun Print

It's a helluva start, being able to recognize what makes you happy.

—LUCILLE BALL

What's a Fun Print? It's your individual, intricate imprint of fun—a crazy cocktail of the types of things that tickle your fun bone. No one has the exact same Fun Print. It's yours and yours alone. Some like golf, some like opera, some like quiet time on the beach, but no one has the same exact combination of what + what + what = FUN.

Take a few minutes around the dinner table to talk this over with your family. Ask them when was the last time they had a ripping good time—not the last time they were supposed to be having fun, but the last time they actually *enjoyed* themselves.

Here's a good question to ask them: when do you forget time? By "forget time," I mean when do you forget your worries, the past, your stressors, that mammoth ever-fattening to-do list—and really *live* in the moment, whether you are engrossed in a task at work or with the kids or doing something you truly enjoy? *Time flies when you are having fun,* as they say, so really pay attention for the next few weeks. Take note of the times the clock takes a bionic whirl, drop-kicking you an hour down life's road. What were you doing then? *That* is fun to you!

You owe it to yourself to stop being a Fun Zombie and to find (or create) your own flavor of fun made just for you and your family.

I trust all joy.   —THEODORE ROETHKE

> **! FUN FACT:**
>
> In a study published in the *Journal of Happiness Studies*, researchers divided events that increase your well-being into intentional acts, like starting a new hobby class, and circumstantial changes, like having a nice, new neighbor move in. They performed three studies on psychology students who recently experienced an increase in well-being. These studies showed that sustainable happiness was possible only through active changes. Intentional changes resulted in a bigger boost in happiness. And those who became happier because they made a change in their lives stayed happy, whereas the ones who became happy by chance found their happiness to be fleeting. Learning how to *make yourself* happy is the only way to true happiness.

Happiness is not something ready made. It comes from your own actions.

          —DALAI LAMA XIV

Easy Peasy Does It

Once you're ready to start folding fun into your life, you might be tempted to try to fill your days with unicorn rides. You can stretch your limits and your budget and reach for the stars, but fun doesn't have to be hard, it doesn't always have to be big, and it doesn't have to be expensive. This is the biggest mistake I see folks make. They make F-U-N so hard. They wait for it. Compartmentalize it. They hoard it and save it for vacations, anniversaries, summer break, treading through life until it's finally time for a little fun. What happens when we do that? We get rusty. We overthink it. We squeeze it tight, choking it, as we say to ourselves, *THIS needs to be really fun—gosh darn it.* Most of the time we suck the fun right out of that special moment, special day, or special been-waiting-all-my-life-for-this trip. If you don't call on it often, fun quickly forgets your name.

Starting today, stop compartmentalizing fun. Don't just concentrate on the big, supposed-to-be-fun moments of your life. Those are great to plan, of course—but sprinkle in a lot of what I like to call Easy Peasy Does Its along the way. Look for simple, tiny, *easy* ways to make your time *right now* a bit more exciting, cheerful, and warm.

Little by little does the trick.   —Aesop

A walk to school with little ones becomes magical with a bottle of bubbles. Krazy Straws always make chocolate milk taste better. Have a long car ride with the kids? Download songs with their names in them. Or if you are close to St. Patrick's Day, Irish music will do the trick. Boring family dinners become richer when you picnic together on the front porch. A night in is made memorable sleeping by the fireplace—in our family we called it *going to the mattresses* because I would actually pull all our mattresses off the box springs and plunk them around the fire—with fireplace hot dogs for dinner and of course roasted marshmallows for dessert.

> *A person who's happy will make others happy.*
>
> —ANNE FRANK

And it's not just for kids. Fun-starved grown-ups can benefit from little Easy Peasy Does Its. Try driving to work a different way for a change of scenery. Or, if you can, walk. When I worked at NBC in Chicago I figured out that the walk home along the lake took as much time as the nauseating, crowded city bus ride. As I walked, baby ducks bobbing on the glistening water ripples behind their mamas, I felt like I was on vacation. It was for only forty minutes, mind you, but instead of just two weeks a year, I found a simple way to have a little slice of vacation nearly every day. If there is a water taxi in your town, take it. What a commute! Or strap on some Rollerblades. Go to a movie at lunchtime. Plan a progressive dinner, where you start dinner at one house and move from house to house, each family hosting a different course, with your neighbors—half the work, twice the fun. Seek out simple ways to make dull moments spellbinding with a bit of FUN, and you and your family will begin enjoying *all* the parts of your days.

Where should you slip in an Easy Peasy Does It? Anywhere you can! The five minutes while breakfast is cooking. The wait at the bus stop. The too-long car ride to the grandparents'. The witching hour before naptime when there is not quite enough time to go somewhere. Look for ways to add a little twist of FUN to lift up the saggy parts of your days.

If you don't know where to start, ask yourself:

What is something we do almost every day and dread?
What times of day are most boring?
Where are the small parcels of our day with not enough time
*   to do something complicated?*
What do we do that is so mindless we have bandwidth for
*   something else?*
When are we stuck? Like home with a napping child or in the
*   car between tight pickups?*

Take those moments, and gather all the other moments you can—find a bit of smiley stuff and squirt it on the yawn-y parts of life.

Get Fun with Funny, Stat!

The most wasted of all days is one without laughter.

—Nicolas Chamfort

When you can't go FUN, reach for FUNny! Funny is fast, and it's just as good as fun, with many of the same benefits.

Not only is funny good for you; it's good for your relationships. When we laugh with one another, a positive bond is created. The bond you create with humor acts as a strong buffer against stress, disagreements, and disappointment. It keeps relationships fresh and exciting. All emotional sharing builds

---

! *FUN FACT:*

Doctors at the Mayo Clinic found that laughter is a huge stress reliever and provides physical benefits. Laughter doesn't just lighten your load mentally; it actually induces physical changes in your body. Laughter stimulates many organs; enhances oxygen intake; stimulates the heart, lungs, and muscles; increases the endorphins released by your brain; and rouses circulation. And, down the road, laughter releases neuropeptides that help fight serious illnesses, relieve pain, lessen depression and anxiety, and make you feel happier.

---

strong and lasting relationship bonds, but sharing laughter and play also adds joy, vitality, and resilience. Not only that, funny is an instant power-struggle interrupter, easing tension and allowing reconnection. It's an effective way to heal resentments, disagreements, and hurts. Plus, funny allows us to be more spontaneous, to let go of inhibitions. We are less defensive. We are free to express what we truly feel, and our deep, genuine emotions rise to the surface.

> *Laughter is an instant vacation.* —MILTON BERLE

Have you ever argued with your spouse in opera? Really. It's worked for me and my husband for almost ten years. Just try it. Betcha can't go more than a minute without falling into fits of laughter. Especially if you are terrible singers like we are!

Imagine *"I don't like how you never take out the trash or empty the dishwasher . . . ,"* in a high, heavy soprano.

It's good for kids to watch you effectively reduce and re-solve conflict by finding funny together. By doing so, you will be teaching them to do the same. Research says—and this is no surprise—how you argue with your spouse is the same way your teen will argue with you. So when you argue—and we *ALL* argue at times—find a way to make your partner giggle. Make it a funny fight.

> *A person without a sense of humor is like a wagon without springs. They are jolted by every pebble on the road.*
>
> —Henry Ward Beecher

And don't just wait for conflict to pour on the funny and fun with your family or your spouse. A recent study from the University of Winnipeg found that the number-one problem facing long-term relationships is not lying or cheating or even money problems; it's boredom. HINT: You are not bored when you are having FUN together. Try pouring some light-heartedness on your marriage. It's worth the effort.

Make Fun a Priority

If you want to put more fun in your days, start by locking in fun FIRST.

This is crazy-hard for us. It feels fickle, foolish—sometimes downright silly to put fun in front of the billion zillion six trillion things we have to do. But, even so, we need to make it a point to make room for fun in our lives. Start saying yes to FUN first, and find some way to muster up a big fat N-O to those things you feel you *should* do that suck up all of your time.

How?

STOP CARING WHAT OTHER PEOPLE THINK

The first step in putting fun first is to stop caring what other people think. My old neighbor once said to me, "Let's be the kind of friends who don't care what each other's house looks like." What freeing words! I was happy to have her pop on over anytime. If I'm caught with a not-so-presentable house, my new go-to line is "We are a messy family. We are okay with that and hope you are too!" It gives me permission to let a good time roll a bit before squashing it with a hafta chore.

SAY NO

Try it. *No.* Louder. *No.* Again. *No.* Then say it to the things you really don't want to do, like reading a four-hundred-page book for a book club you don't enjoy. Like spending yet another evening with people who talk endlessly about their kids and never ask you once about yours. Like that umpteenth phone call from that whiny relative who is just calling to complain and steal your joy. Trust me. It gets easier with practice!

LEARN TO LET GO

Let go of that extra cello lesson or family favor or whatever it is that gobbles up your time, leaving you no time for fun. This goes double for all those volunteer gigs complete with oodles of drama. You know the kind I mean, with dozens of e-mails debating the exact color blue for the fund-raiser decorations. My goodness. Who has time for all that? You don't. Not if you want to put more fun in your days.

START CENTERING YOUR DAY AROUND FUN

Move your schedule around to take advantage of fleeting FUN. This might mean having the kids come home for their lunch hour to knock out their homework so that you can go to a concert together that night. Or maybe everyone does an extra thirty minutes of chores each weekday evening so that you can have your Saturday free for fantastic FUN. Or hire a teen driver for your kids' sports carpools on Thursday nights so you can head downtown with the hubby for a romantic dinner or drinks with friends.

START ADVANCE PLANNING FOR FUN

Block your time and create your own fun strategy for your family. Do you know you're going to have a free hour together between soccer games tomorrow? Make that time count with some advance planning and activities on the ready, like maybe a special roadside picnic and a football.

The wicked envy and hate; it is their way of admiring.

—VICTOR HUGO

Avoid No-Fun Zones

To avoid places and people that suck your energy:

REROUTE YOUR DAY

Avoid uncomfortable people or situations with a strategic switch. Hit the late strength class or take an earlier train to work if it means being around more positive folks or at least avoiding the negative ones. Courting a new crowd may even give you a chance to make new friends.

AVOID TOXIC PEOPLE

If you find serenity and happiness, they may be jealous. Be happy anyway.

—MOTHER TERESA

Energy Vampires are out there and are often not too far away. They are tucked tight in your family, on your tennis team, at work, and in your book club. We all know them. No square inch of earth is exempt. And if you're not careful, not only can Energy Vampires rob your joy; they can also make you sick. In a study published in the journal *Proceedings of the National Academy of Sciences*, scientists at UCLA's School of Medicine found that negative social interactions can lead to a host of illnesses, from cancer to heart disease to high blood pressure. The study gives solid grounding to the evidence that being upbeat and positive—and surrounding yourself with people who are not competitive or toxic—may be one way to avoid getting sick and, most important, *stay happy*. Identify the people in your life who bring you down. By avoiding them, you will up the good times in life.

LOOK JUST BEYOND YOUR COMFORT ZONE

The cave you fear to enter holds the treasure you seek.

—JOSEPH CAMPBELL

It's easy to quit trying new things, meeting new people, or opening your eyes to fun, fresh adventure. *Do not turn away from something you want to do because you are afraid.* Now, I'm not suggesting you jump out of an airplane—although I've done it, and let me tell you, hanging off the wing of an airplane ready to free-fall is not exactly the comfort zone. If it's not dangerous (and I am talking personal safety, like trying to out-run a freight train), do it, even if it makes you uncomfortable—*especially* if it makes you uncomfortable. Kick through that wall of fear. It gets easier every time you do. Learning how to stop playing it safe is one way to unlock more fun in your life.

> *Boldness be my friend.*   —WILLIAM SHAKESPEARE

REFRAME THE DAY

If I'm frazzled or blue or frustrated, or if I'm even just hit with a moment of bitter boredom, I think, *What's the worst thing that could be happening to me right now?* The scenario—whether it's a sick child, homelessness, blindness—gets me to appreciate the dull moment I was bumping through in my current life stream. I think, *Wow, if I was there in bleak despair and then I was drop-kicked back into this moment, how darn happy would I be?* It's a great trick to keep at the ready when you feel things aren't going your way and your mind starts to creep on over to the dark side. It's a simple strategy that reminds us things can always be worse and forces us to be grateful for each and every moment.

> *It is impossible to feel grateful and depressed in the same moment.*
>
>   —NAOMI WILLIAMS

STAY IN THE PRESENT

When the sky explodes into vibrant color or I spot a fantastically happy field of sunflowers on a country back road, I pause the patter of my thought track and really breathe it in. If my girls are in the car with me and I see something spectacular, I will say to them, "Put it in your heart." I initially started pointing these things out to the girls to make our days together more fun but then added the *put it in your heart* in hopes they would start to build a beauty arsenal to get them through tough times they may have to face later in life. They loved it when they were little and would look at whatever spontaneous discovery I spotted along our way wide-eyed. Of course now that they are teens, they mock me, saying, "Let me just get surgery, open my heart, and slide that one in, Momma." But I tell ya, they look every time. And every once in a while, they'll spot something I didn't catch, and before they can stop themselves they'll say, "Look, Momma. Put it in your heart." And I do. Every time.

> *Realize deeply that the present moment is all you ever have.*
> *Make the NOW the primary focus of your life.*
>
> —ECKHART TOLLE

Pinch yourself every once in a while. Look around and say, "I am here in the *now*," and let your life unfold from there. It's easy to just go through the motions of the day and forget to look around and really absorb the moment. This trick will also deepen the time you spend with your children. More than anything, your kids want you to be you with them—you in this moment, not you thinking of a hundred million other things.

ENJOY. IT'S A VERB.

As you look to fold more fun throughout your days, remember it's not just about making time great; it's about actively making a point to enJOY the time you have. EnJOY is a verb. It means to purposely find joy in all your moments. It's not always *what* you do—it's *how* you do it. Act on fun today in little and big chunks and your life will change.

Ways to Trick Yourself into Putting Fun First

MAKE A DATE

Schedule your fun like you would an important work appointment, or dentist or doctor's appointment.

INVITE FRIENDS

I would do this on museum days with the girls. We had a little system where I would snag them after kindergarten and preschool and head down to the city for a museum half day. Afraid I would sneak in a couple of household chores first and that precious window for fun would slam closed, I'd let them invite a friend (in advance) so I was on somebody else's schedule and on the hook.

PACK LUNCHES

If you are picking the kids up from school before an outing, don't come home first, where too many kill-the-day distractions loom. Pack a sack lunch or dinner and beeline for good times. I find eating in the car or on a quick picnic saves time, and everyone shows up for the fun you have planned fully energized.

PROMISE THE KIDS

Promise the kids a fun outing—and they surely won't let you forget.

PAY IT FORWARD

Put your money where your mouth is and buy the tickets or sign up for the lessons or whatever the fun is in advance. Then you are stuck—in a good way!

MAKE A BUCKET LIST

We try to do this every year at the beginning of summer. We put our ideas on slips of paper and put all the slips inside a plastic sand bucket. On days together we pull out a task and throw it away once completed. The goal is to empty the bucket before school starts. PS: You don't have to wait until summer to make a bucket list. Any time is a good time.

BLOOM WHERE YOU ARE PLANTED

Things might not be perfect right here, right now (if you are waiting for perfectly perfect, you'll wait a long, long time). Maybe you are stuck at home on Friday nights because you don't have a vehicle. Invite a neighbor over to play cards. It's easy to feel victimized, bored, and lonely—but in the end it's up to *you* to make the most fun with what you have right now by finding simple ways to bloom where you are planted.

Create Your Happy Place: Happy Home, Happy Family

A recent Gallup poll says 96 percent of people say family is the most important thing in their lives. So how do you create a happy family? By creating a happy home.

No other success can compensate for failure in the home.

—DAVID O. MCKAY

MY HOUSE RULES

Enjoy One Another

Enjoy one another's company. Be happy when you see one another—first thing in the morning or right after school or between sports and plans. Find ways to show how excited you are to see one another. This is important these days as family schedules get crazier and crazier and we have less time to spend together.

Celebrate Family History

Happy families love who they are because they love where they've come from—they have a sense of sharing lives. Researchers at Emory University say the single most important thing you can do for your family is to develop a strong family narrative. Share those family stories with your kids—the funny stories, stories about hard times, stories about how they were born, stories that show them how much you love them— stories about how you've become the family you are today.

Make Time for Family Dinner—or Look for a Twist

You hear it again and again—you can't say enough about the benefits of the family dinner. Studies show that children who eat dinner with their families are less likely to drink, do drugs, commit suicide, or get pregnant, and they have larger vocabularies, better manners, healthier diets, and higher self-esteem. But here is something you may not have heard: it turns out that the family dinner conversation—the productive part—lasts only about ten minutes. So that's good news if you don't have time to have family dinner every night. I say re-create it in other parts of the day: breakfast, Saturday lunch, or even tea. Get creative!

> *The ache for home lives in all of us, the safe place where we can go as we are and not be questioned.*
>
> —MAYA ANGELOU

Mom and Dad Come First

If Mom and Dad are both in the home, they are the center of a happy family, so give yourselves permission to strengthen that relationship. You not only set the tone for your family; you also set an example. This is true even for parents who are no longer together—work on that relationship, make it a positive, cooperative relationship no matter what your circumstances. It'll pay dividends when it comes to the kids and how they feel about their family and themselves.

Create a Light House

To create a light, "life is great" vibe at home, look for ways to laugh, even in life's most frustrating moments: the spilled orange juice, the ripped pants. When those things happen, you have a choice: get flustered, get mad, or simply laugh it off and give everyone permission to laugh with you.

Create a No-Stress Zone for Your Family

Do you know what kids want most from their parents? It's not money or things or even more time spent together. According to the Families and Work Institute, a child's number-one wish is that their parents are less tired and less stressed when they are with them. So, create a stress-free zone at home. Leave your troubles, worries, gripes, and stressors on the doorstep.

Create Fun Zones at Home

Create fun zones at home—places designated for fun. Not only will your children have fun with *you*; they will also be more apt to have friends over—a fantastic way to really be a part of your children's lives. For younger kids, I love a destruction-proof art space in the crappiest corner of your house, a science lab, or a costume corner set up for creative play. For older kids, maybe it's a music room with karaoke, a graffiti wall they are allowed to sign, bongo drums, or a game room with family favorites like Ping-Pong.

> **! FUN FACT:**
>
> According to the *American Journal of Play*, social play allows children to become more creative and more adept at explaining meaning verbally, more successful at manipulating different symbol systems, and more confident when experimenting with new activities.

Wear Your Heart on Your Sleeve

Hug, cuddle, tickle, touch, and tell your family you love them, early, often, every day.

Be Present with Your Children

Make sure you are carving out time to really absorb and *be* with your child. They want *you*—not you thinking of the umpteen million things you have to do.

Say the Same Thing Every Night Before They Go to Sleep

Research tells us that kids learn by repetition—they remember what they hear again and again. So come up with a family mantra and say it again and again and again. If you don't know what to say, borrow ours. We say, "I love you all that there is—more than there is, just because you are [name]," every (okay, most) nights before bed. Let your positive, loving thoughts be the last words your children hear every night.

Be Positive, Especially When Times Are Tough

Be positive. Tough times are going to come. No family is immune. But tough times don't seem so scary to kids when Mom and Dad handle it in stride. Keep your cool.

Adapt/Change

Family is fluid. Kids grow up, interests change, needs change, and our way of communicating changes, so it's important that we are ready and willing to change along with it.

What to Have on Hand for
Instant Fun Anytime

Little things make big things happen.   —JOHN WOODEN

Krazy Straws make everything taste better. Keep a cupful on your kitchen counter!

Food coloring is magic—it turns thirsty carnations into magical rainbows. Just add a couple of drops to vase water and presto!

Bubbles are so fun! Keep a jar in your car and one in your purse to make a few minutes' wait or some downtime poppy! Bubbles are the quickest way to make a walk from one place to the other FUN. Just try it with your little ones. You can barely finish blowing before they start popping them.

Sidewalk chalk makes any chunk of sidewalk (and the hands that hold it) happy.

Sunglasses make every card game exciting. Wearing them while you play gives everyone that fun, Hollywood poker-ish vibe. I keep a container of them in our game room. We adults have been known to wear them too. My daughter Ava used to sleep with a pair when she was two or three. Made bedtime much, much cooler.

Play-Doh is fantastic for a long plane ride. Peels right off of the tray—a wipe will make sure you've gotten it all. Throw away once you land.

Instamatic cameras are irresistible. And what teen can resist a fun picture to display? Fun to take and share. I bring mine to volleyball games and hand them out in the stands.

A bouquet of colorful Sharpie markers makes all homework more fun. I keep a couple of bouquets in Mason jars on our homework area at home. Stock up at back-to-school time when they are crazy-cheap.

Dice are awesome. So easy to slip in a pocket or purse—I keep a handful on the console of my Suburban. Instant fun anytime.

A deck of cards is great. Who doesn't like to play cards? You can play anytime, anywhere—in the doctor's office, even on an airport floor. Have on hand for Go Fish, War, Rummy, Hearts.

Duct tape makes a long car ride or any downtime more fun. Make purses, eyeglass cases, bracelets— the possibilities are endless.

Homemade road-trip T-shirts with fun vacation slogans make a trip more fun. Two of ours? The Road Less Traveled and The Rush to Rushmore.

Sprinkles make everything from ice cream to French toast more exciting. Give it a shake.

Happiness depends upon ourselves. —ARISTOTLE

You've cleared the way, but I know what you are thinking: *if only you had a magical list of things to do with your family anytime, anywhere, again and again. They have to be fast, be simple, not cost a fortune—and, of course, be packed with FUN.*

You got it. Up next: *lots* to do in section two!

Section Two

CHAPTER THREE

Giggly Times

Enjoy the little things, for one day you may look back and realize they were the big things.

—ROBERT BRAULT

You know my prescription, always—keep it simple, silly. So I've scribbled out what I call my Easy Peasy Does Its—simple, fantastic ways to put tons of family fun into bits of days.

Add a Dose of Humor to Your Days

From there to here, from here to there, funny things are everywhere.

—DR. SEUSS

TURN YOUR HOUSE INTO A COMEDY CLUB

Let the kids spend the day finding jokes and writing down their material. Check out joke books from the library. Google jokes together. Or even buy joke books in advance on Amazon.com. Then, one at a time, get up to the "mic" and try your jokes out on the crowd. Any mic will do—a toy mic, a banana, an empty toilet paper roll. I like to jazz things up with fake mustaches, old ties, sunglasses, and decorated hats. An old shower curtain makes a great stage backdrop. Drumsticks can be fun for audience members to make a ta-dum-dum sound effect for favored jokes. Big wholesome fun for grown-ups and kids alike on a wintry evening at home, and the best part is everyone is *together.*

Ages: 3–8   *Time:* 40 magical minutes

THE FUNNIES

Tuck comics in the seat-back pockets of your car if you do a lot of carting around town. A giggle and a snort are only a reach away.

Ages: 8–10   *Time:* A car ride

DASH AND LAUGH

Velcro a joke-a-day calendar onto your dashboard and let the kids take turns leading the carpool laugh-a-thon.

Ages: 7–10   *Time:* 30 seconds

GO TO A COMEDY CLUB

If you have a comedy club that allows children, go!

Ages: 12 and up   *Time:* An evening

CLOWNING AROUND TOWN

Try a clowning class—yep, they have those. Look to acting studios, community colleges, and comedy troupes that offer classes. Or create your own clowning academy—check out some clowning books at the library and study up on clowning YouTube videos.

Ages: 3–8   *Time:* 40 magical minutes

JOKE ROUND-ROBIN AT DINNERTIME

Host joke contests at dinnertime or save up jokes for little ones at bath time. Throw some riddles into the mix too. They keep dinnertime jumping and little brains thumping.

Ages: 5 and up   *Time:* Dinner hour, bath time, or a giggly wake-up call

COMEDY MOVIE NIGHT

Declare Sunday nights comedy movie night and scare off the dread of Monday morning. My family does this when the long winters start to drag.

Ages: 8 and up   *Time:* 90 minutes

PLAY FUNNY VIDEOS

When I was working in the creative department of a television station, I would invite the producers and designers on my team to bring funny YouTube videos to our weekly meeting. It lightened the mood, gave us all something to look forward to, and fostered a productive, creative spirit. Save up those funny videos you find on Facebook or on YouTube to kick off dinner (before you come to the table) or a family game night. Or just save one for a rough winter morning before everyone is off to school and work.

Ages: Any   *Time:* 2–20 minutes

SHHH! WHAT'S SO FUNNY?

Look for private jokes in your family; private stories and jokes bind us together. When something funny happens or when someone in the family says something funny, bring it up again and again until it becomes a running family joke.

Ages: All   *Time:* Seconds

PLAY *MAKE ME LAUGH*

Remember the hit show in the seventies? It's all about not laughing, but in the end, you can't help but laugh your butt off. Set the timer—a minute is good. Two people sit face-to-face. The joker's job is to make the other person laugh, by any means necessary. The player's job is to remain as straight-faced as possible. Can you go a full minute without cracking a smile? It's fun to find out.

Ages: 4–12   *Time:* 1 minute

HAVE A JOKE-WRITING CONTEST

And try out the winners at dinner, in the car, or when you're just hanging out after homework in the evening.

Ages: 8–13   *Time:* 20 minutes plus

> *We cannot really love anybody with whom we never laugh.*
>
> —AGNES REPPLIER

MEET FUNNY HALFWAY—ALWAYS, ALWAYS, ALWAYS

LOL! The secret to finding something funny is always being willing. Lighten up and laugh at the littlest things. You'll find your family laughing with you.

Ages: Any   *Time:* Seconds

> **❗ FUN FACT:**
>
> According to research presented at the Economic and Social Research Council's Festival of Social Science, joking with your toddler helps set them up for social success. When parents joke and pretend, it gives young kids the tools to think creatively, make friends, and manage stress.

ENCOURAGE SILLY GAMES

Challenge the kids to a popcorn or M&M'S toss, flinging either into happy open mouths. Simple, silly, and sure to bring giggles.

Ages: 5–14   *Time:* 5 minutes

CHEAP TRICK: FIND FUNNY PROPS

Lighten the mood during homework hour, at breakfast, or on a long car ride with funny props. Mustaches, oversized sunglasses, and wax lips lighten the mood and can get lots of laughs, especially with little ones.

Ages: 2 and up   *Time:* Seconds

▼▼▼▼▼▼▼▼▼▼▼▼▼▼▼▼▼▼▼▼▼▼▼▼▼▼▼▼▼▼▼▼

Fun from the Field

For Erin P., using a funny prop means wearing a funky netting hat with spiders come Halloween time as she carpools her kids to and fro. Her little ones beg her to wear it—they love spotting the spiders along the way.

▲▲▲▲▲▲▲▲▲▲▲▲▲▲▲▲▲▲▲▲▲▲▲▲▲▲▲▲▲▲▲▲

FUNNY FRIDGE

Is your refrigerator running—on funny? Print out funny snips and sayings or one-page cartoons and stick them on the fridge for all to enjoy. Swap in new funnies each week. You can even let the kids take turns tacking up their favorite laughs.

Ages: All   *Time:* 15 minutes

DECLARE IT PRACTICAL JOKE WEEK

Grab some whoopee cushions and bug ice cubes. Declare it practical joke week at home and let the zingers fly.

Ages: 4–12   *Time:* A funny-filled week

KNOCK KNOCK!

Take the edge of a piece of soap and write your best knock-knock jokes on the kids' bathroom mirror before they wake up.

Ages: Any   *Time:* Seconds

FIND A FUNNY RHYME

Challenge your family to combine their best one-liners with a progressive punny poem. Cut a grocery bag into long, skinny strips and tape to the wall of your breakfast nook or mudroom—someplace everyone gathers. You go first with that first funny line, then challenge the rest of the gang to keep adding to the poem as the week goes by.

Ages: Any   *Time:* A couple of days to a week

☞ **Take Note!**

Looking for a funny read for little ones? Check out *Walter the Farting Dog* by William Kotzwinkle and Glenn Murray.

A PLACE FOR FUNNY

Get them laughing at the breakfast table. Cut the funny section of the newspaper into a place-mat-sized rectangle or assemble some of the funnier Facebook comic strips. Laminate your place mat with a laminating machine or self-adhesive sheets—even packing tape does the trick in a pinch.

Ages: Any   *Time:* 30 minutes

GALVANIZE THOSE FUNNY FAMILY QUOTES

When you stumble upon the hilarious in life, hang it up. Write those funny family lines on a chalkboard, frame them, or make a plaque out of them with any kind of letters. Hang your funny reminder where everyone can see it.

Ages: Any   *Time:* 30 minutes

MAD LIBS

Between rounds of homework do a quick Mad Lib with the kids. Remember Mad Libs? Fun(ny) with words is the best kind of fun, and it makes for good learning too.

Ages: 6–10   *Time:* 20 minutes

You don't stop laughing because you grow old. You grow old because you stop laughing.

—MICHAEL PRITCHARD

CHAPTER FOUR

Simple Times

What to Do When There's Nothing to Do

*The two enemies of human happiness are pain and
boredom.*

—Arthur Schopenhauer

BUG HUNT

Send the kids on a bug hunt! I discovered how fun this
little game can be when I threw a science birthday party for
my oldest daughter, Juliana, when she was in kindergarten. To
kill time while we were waiting for everyone to arrive, I sent
the kids on a bug hunt. I hid a few little plastic bugs in the
backyard, but they ended up finding lots of live little guys as
well. It was such a big hit, I had a hard time getting them to go
on to the real science activities I had planned. Buy little bug

carriers or jars with holes poked in the lid and have fun collecting and releasing.

Ages: 2–6   *Time:* 15 minutes plus

TRAVEL THE WORLD WITHOUT LEAVING THE NEIGHBORHOOD

Stuck home on spring break? Who says you have to travel to a foreign country to tour the world? Set up a progressive dinner with your neighbors. Each house hosts a country with special food, games, and activities. Guests go around the world traveling from house to house. Challenge guests to pick up four new words in a different language and learn new cultural facts to share at each delicious stop. Decorate with foreign flags and cultural items from your chosen country.

Ages: Any   *Time:* An evening

GLOW-IN-THE-DARK DINNER

Turn off the lights, stick glow-in-the-dark stars on the ceiling, and have a starlight dinner with foods that remind you of the night. You can serve black foods like black bean soup, black olives, eggplant, or blackberry salad. Or make StarKist tuna casserole and serve MoonPies, Milky Way bars, or gummy night crawlers for dessert. Just a STARter—but you get the picture. Add glow-stick bouquets in glow-in-the-dark Mason jars for extra fun. Or take the lightbulbs out of the chandelier and replace with black lightbulbs for a glowy grub fest.

Ages: Any   *Time:* Dinner hour

A WORD PARADE

Have the kids dress up as their favorite word—"luminous," "studious," "zany"—and parade around the house or neighborhood.

Ages: 5–8   *Time:* 40 minutes

FAMILY MOVIES

Make your own family movie. Smartphones and simple editing software like iMovie or Final Cut Express make it easy.

Ages: 8 and up   *Time:* Varies

FAMILY PLAY

It's lots of fun to play with a play. Create a family play for the holiday season or any time of year. Have fun writing a script, or find one on the Internet. Build a set, simple or extravagant. Audition your actors, whether they are people or stuffed animals and dolls. Make costumes out of scrap material and select music and sound effects on the computer.

Ages: 6–9   *Time:* 1 week

FASHION SHOW

Create runway magic with a fashion show at home. You can use live models or dolls and stuffed animals to showcase the clothes. Create your own fashion designs with scraps of fabric.

Ages: 6–8   *Time:* 1 week

MAKE YOUR OWN STUFFED ANIMALS

Have the kids make their own stuffed animals with fuzzy fabric or felt, staplers, and some kind of stuffing like cotton filling—even crumpled newspaper works. Just cut fabric into your animal shape and staple the edges, leaving a hand-hole for stuffing. Stuff with crumpled newspaper or filling and staple the hole closed. Glue on buttons for noses and eyes.

Ages: 2–6   *Time:* 1 hour

PITCH A TENT IN THE BACKYARD

A backyard tent makes both day and night more fun. Camp out for the night pretending you are the last people on earth—or the first. Or pretend you've all run away from home.

Ages: Any   *Time:* Overnight, or just long (and late) enough

OPEN A FAMILY RESTAURANT

Invite the neighbors—or just a group of the kids' friends— to dine at Chez Vous. Free of charge, of course. Shake out the tablecloths, set up the card tables, make homemade restaurant menus, and serve up some simple entrées to order. Hire the kids to play waiter and waitress. Cute bow ties, little notepads, and aprons will help them play the part. Bonus if you have a musician in your house to tickle the ivories or fiddle a homegrown tune! Why not?

Ages: 3 and up   *Time:* A few hours

WHERE'S TEDDY?

Who needs Christmastime for the Elf on the Shelf? Have a little fun with your kids by hiding a family mascot (stuffed animal) in crazy, unexpected places around the house, in the car, or in your child's locker at school. Make it a family affair, with each family member taking a day to hide it in a random spot, like the chandelier above the dinner table.

Ages: 5–9   *Time:* Ongoing fun

☞ Take Note!

What the . . . ?! Kids not playing with the toys *right in front of them*? Here is my number-one tip for getting the most from your toys: *rotate them*. I did this frequently when my girls were young, swapping toys and setups from their bedrooms to the toy room or a little room we had on the main floor. My husband used to question the extra work until he saw how excited they were to see fresh toys (not new, just mixed up) and how they would play and play and play in their new (to them) play space.

PAINT THE BASEMENT

Okay, not for the faint of heart parent, but perfect for the family who doesn't mind a mess for the sake of fun *and* has a scrappy play basement. Ask the kids if they want to paint the basement. "Yes, yes, yes!" they will say—because really, what could be more fun? Make it a project with design meetings to decide the colors, a field trip to the store to get paint and brushes, and of course, lots of fun time painting, painting, painting. And more painting and more painting. Their friends can even come by to join in on the fun. Candy-apple red with white stripes? Bright turquoise with yellow dots? Or flowers that grow to the sky? The kids will be so proud of their hand-work and will love playing in a room they created as their own.

Ages: 5 and up   *Time:* A couple of weeks

Bozzo Family Fun File

We spent such a wonderful summer painting the Bozzo basement. Color me happy with purple, purple, and more purple, with silver swizzles, of course.

☞ **Take Note!**

What the . . . ?! No interest in taking on such a drastic (messy) project as painting the basement? Instead, invite little visitors to leave a handprint on a section of wall. Keep it neat by squeezing a little paint on a paper plate, then have the little one dip his or her hand in the paint and gently press it onto the wall. Keep wipes on hand for a quick-before-you-get-paint-on-anything-else wipe-down. Limited appetite for mess? Use washable paints and paint the side of the garage. When you're ready for a clean slate, just turn on the hose. Fun that runs!

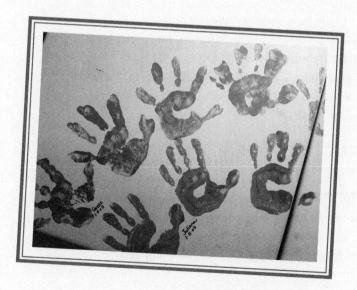

KARAOKE

Pick up a karaoke machine, or better yet, make a home-made version with poster board, write out the lyrics, and take turns belting out the songs.

Ages: Any   *Time:* 1 hour plus

CAR WASH

Pull out the wash buckets, sponges, and towels, and have the kids wash the car in their swimsuits. Of course, the hose is the best part. Crank up the song "Car Wash" by Rose Royce and dance away the dirt.

Ages: 4 and up   *Time:* A lazy summer afternoon

FORTS

This is definitely not new but a good reminder. Kids love building forts. Put out the blankets, sheets, and pillows, and let them build a village of fun. Keep it up all week in the name of play. Who cares about the mess?

Ages: 3–8   *Time:* 30 minutes to build for as long as you decide to play!

CREATE AN OUTDOOR SCAVENGER HUNT

What do you do when you have time to kill with a little one? Give them a brown lunch bag and a list of pictures of things to find—a red leaf, an acorn, a pinecone—and go on an outdoor scavenger hunt.

Ages: 2–5   *Time:* As long as you need

Fun from the Field

Jen M. says an outdoor scavenger hunt was the perfect thing to make the bewitching time between when her kids woke up from their nap and when they could start the nighttime routine more fun.

GO DOWN TO THE FARM

Spend the day at a local farm and show kids that vegetables don't come from the grocery store.

Ages: 2 and up   ***Time:*** A couple of hours

TAKE LITTLE ONES TO A HIGH SCHOOL SPORTING EVENT, CONCERT, OR PLAY

Little ones find big fun when attending high school events—the bigger gym, the bigger kids, the bigger crowds. So take advantage of free, or at the very least very cheap, admission to that nighttime high school game, play, or concert.

Ages: 4 and up   *Time:* A fun evening or afternoon

> **! FUN FACT:**
>
> Is boredom bad for your health? It very well could be. According to *Psychology Today*, researchers found bored people are 2.5 times more likely to die of a heart problem. That's about how much more likely a smoker is to develop coronary heart disease than a nonsmoker, according to the American Heart Association.

Free Fun

I'm going to keep having fun every day I have left. Because there's no other way to play it.

—RANDY PAUSCH

WE LIKE BIKING

Decorate bikes with streamers and go on a family bike ride. If your kids are too little for a long family ride, invest in or borrow a tandem attachment for your bike so they can pedal for as long or as little as they want.

Ages: 4–15   *Time:* 1 hour for setup, and you decide the ride!

Bozzo Family Fun File

I remember biking around our shiny new neighborhood with my parents. I was still on training wheels, collecting friends along the way. In the end, we had a fun little parade—quite a memory for me still today, and something I've passed on to my girls.

 Take Note!

Looking for a fantastic way to take in a new city? Try a bike tour. It's a great way to get outside, get moving, and learn about a new place.

A TAD FUN

Spend a warm spring afternoon looking for tadpoles at a nearby forest preserve.

Ages: 3–8   *Time:* 1 hour

VOLLEYBALL FUN

Next time you're on a family trip or hanging out with extended family, throw a backyard volleyball tournament. One way to distract the opponents: keep them laughing at you. Have each team of two come up with a funny name and even funnier outfit.

Ages: All   *Time:* Depending on the number of players, 1–3 days

A LEAGUE OF YOUR OWN

Create fun on the field for the next family football game (or any game) by making your own jersey. Eye black optional. Find a field at night and play under the lights for big added effect.

Ages: All   *Time:* 40 minutes

Bozzo Family Fun File

One summer night we went to watch my husband play softball under the lights. At the end of the game, my friend Shanda's three boys excitedly asked my husband if he would pitch to them so they could have a chance to bat under the lights. Of course the girls joined in too. About half a second later, we had a line of about twenty very excited children all waiting to take a swing under the lights. Better than Disneyland!

WALK

The daily walk to school can be magical. Little ones start out the day with your full attention, a bit of exercise, and adventure. Walk with your children whenever you can, and even look for a different way to walk to school. Or invite a special guest star like a friend from across town or a special relative. Have them map out a new course complete with a hand-drawn map. Bring along a compass for good measure, or equip the crew with (toy) binoculars for spotting new discoveries.

Ages: All   *Time:* Minutes

▼▼

Fun from the Field

Want to make a usual walk a little more exciting for the kids? Katrine R.'s family likes to take walks in the nearby woods. One day her father took her children to the woods and brought a portable cooking pot and made hot dogs for them among the trees in the middle of the winter. They loved it!

▲▲

DINNER AND A MOVIE

Catch a family movie together on TV. Make it a theme with a movie menu. Think Popsicles for *Frozen*. S'mores for *Ghostbusters*. A cheese platter for *Ratatouille*. Tea sandwiches for *Alice in Wonderland*. For an extra helping of fun, let the kids dress up as their favorite characters.

Ages: All   *Time:* An evening or dinner hour

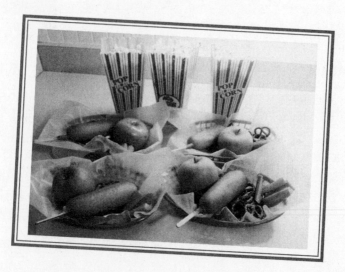

TRY A NEW HAT ON FOR SIZE

Take those old hats out of the closet and paint and decorate with buttons, sequins—anything you might have around the house.

Ages: 3–11   *Time:* 40 minutes

☞ **Take Note!**

Looking for a fun read to top this hat activity for the younger ones? Turn to the classic *Caps for Sale* by Esphyr Slobodkina.

It is your circus and these are your monkeys.

—TWIST ON AN OLD POLISH PROVERB

WADE THROUGH THE PUDDLES AFTER A RAIN

Stuck inside on a rainy day? Nonsense. Put your boots on and slosh your way through the slippery streets. Pretend the street is a river you have to forge. Dance in the rain. If you have a lot of time, make your own umbrella with oilcloth and an old umbrella and save it for the next rainy day. You can find directions on the Internet or at most craft and fabric stores. Or check out *One-Yard Wonders* by Rebecca Yaker and Patricia Hoskins.

Ages: 3–5   *Time:* 30 minutes

RED-LINE READY

If your local city offers a rail, take your little ones on a train ride. They usually ride free on weekends and many times on weekdays too. For us, it's just a way to get from here to there, but to them the ride *is* the adventure. Make it an adventure with rail games like Spot Something Red or Looking for Landmarks, or just admire the city art whizzing past your window together.

Ages: 3 and up   *Time:* Varies

SCATTER PENNIES IN THE PARK

Who needs a pool to dive for pennies? Okay, so maybe this one isn't free, but it'll only cost you a handful of pennies. Do you remember how exciting it was to find coins in the park? Next time you are out and about, secretly scatter a few coins and watch the kids' excitement.

Ages: 3–8   *Time:* 30 minutes

POST-IT LOVE NOTES

Love notes are free, and everyone can use a surprise hello or an encouraging word. Leave Post-it notes for your kids in surprising places like their closet, bedpost, or drawer. You never know how your words can make someone's day.

Ages: 7 and up   *Time:* Seconds

JUNIOR RANGER BADGES

Junior Ranger badges are the *best*. And they are free. Little ones can earn them at most national parks by completing a list of tasks like spotting footprints, finding a fossil, identifying a type of leaf, or describing a wetland. No plans to visit a park?

Put together your own badge requirements and let the kids earn a nature badge at home. Visit the National Park Service website (www.NPS.gov) for inspiration.

Ages: 5–7   **Time:** About 1 hour

LITTLE VILLAGE FUN

Save up all your grocery containers—milk jugs, orange juice containers, cereal boxes, peanut butter jars—along with grocery bags and old receipts. Set up a grocery store for the kids in the basement, toy room, or garage with a toy or old cash register and cart. Change the game up quickly by adding a post office and a pet store with envelopes, paper, and stuffed animals.

Ages: 2–5   **Time:** An afternoon

Sunday Funday

Remember when Sunday stretched into Monday?

Sunday clears away the rust of the whole week.

—Joseph Addison

START A PROJECT TOGETHER

Start a Sunday project. Select something you can look forward to working on together all week. Time spent being together quietly working toward a common end and learning a new skill is great bonding time. Build a dollhouse, or renovate an old one by adding wallpaper, scraps of carpet, miniature chandeliers, and furniture. Build a birdhouse. Or a model plane. Collect stamps, make plans to redecorate a bedroom, or sew a piece of clothing together.

Ages: 8–12   *Time:* Leisurely Sunday afternoons spent together

SUNDAY DINNER

Shake out your grandmother's tablecloth and bring back the traditional Sunday dinner in your home, inviting extended family or honorary family to dine with you at three p.m. What about turkey and stuffing? Or mashed potatoes and a roast? Traditional foods make your meal rich. Follow up with conversation in the parlor or playing cards on the back porch.

Ages: All   *Time:* An afternoon

SUNDAY SUNDAE

Set up a Sunday sundae ice cream bar to celebrate this special day. Easy and fun to do—just grab some tubs of ice cream, or even better, make your own with an ice cream machine. For added fun buy the Ice Cream Ball. You make ice cream with it by adding ingredients inside the ball, including ice, and shaking it, tossing it, and passing it until you have— voilà—ice cream! Line up your favorite toppings—sprinkles, chocolate chips, raisins, nuts, whipped cream, and cherries. Some historians say the sundae was actually invented when blue laws outlawed the selling of ice cream sodas on Sunday, so it's a perfect treat for this day!

Ages: All   *Time:* 1 hour

SET UP A SUNDAY AFTERNOON TEA

Teatime is an honored tradition where you sip time together. Make it an afternoon of fun, setting up the tea table and a tiny stuffed animal or doll table. Grab your favorite toy china or pick up an eclectic set at Goodwill. Doilies and a lace tablecloth make it more formal. So do fancy hats and crazy shoes. Make tea sandwiches. Hot chocolate with mini marshmallows is a hit with kids. Make it a tea party by inviting friends. Try your hand at calligraphy for a formal and fun invite. Or make your own tablecloth with a plain sheet and Sharpie markers or paint pens.

Ages: 5–11   *Time:* A couple of hours

 Take Note!

Looking for a read-along for fancy little ones? *Fancy Nancy: Tea Parties* by Jane O'Connor fits this activity to a T.

CHAPTER FIVE

Good Times

Volunteering Family Fun

To ease another's heartache is to forget one's own.

—Abraham Lincoln

FIND SOME PEN PALS

Write letters to shut-ins or make cards for folks at the hospital or a nursing home. Have the kids come in costume and prepare a little skit to entertain the folks while they are there.

Ages: 6–15   *Time:* Minutes

TOY DRIVE

Have the kids go through their toys and set up a toy drive for your local family shelter. Call first to see if they are accepting toys and what kinds work best. Then set up a time to deliver the toys and play with the kids.

Ages: 5 and up   *Time:* An afternoon

▼▼▼▼▼▼▼▼▼▼▼▼▼▼▼▼▼▼▼▼▼▼▼▼▼▼▼▼▼▼▼▼

Fun from the Field

Julie L. and her kids collect toys for their local children's hospital. She says kids light up when the gifts are brought in. She's even seen many parents cry because folks have done something kind for their children. Many families are financially burdened with medical expenses and often children who are in the hospital over the holidays have chronic sickness, so the toys mean so much to them.

▲▲▲▲▲▲▲▲▲▲▲▲▲▲▲▲▲▲▲▲▲▲▲▲▲▲▲▲▲▲▲▲

 Take Note!

Five- to eight-year-olds will love a book my grandmother gave me, *The Best-Loved Doll* by Rebecca Caudill, which beautifully captures the love children have for a special toy.

Random-Acts-of-Kindness Fun

For it is in giving that we receive.   —FRANCIS OF ASSISI

SURPRISE AN OLDER NEIGHBOR WITH A BIRTHDAY CAKE

Arrange with a relative to surprise an older neighbor on her birthday with a surprise birthday party. You bring the party to her—parade the kids up to the house in birthday hats, carrying balloons and trumpeting noisemakers. Ring the door-bell and yell "surprise." Head to the backyard for cake and lemonade and time spent together.

Ages: Any   *Time:* An afternoon

LEAVE FLOWERS ON A NEIGHBOR'S DOORSTEP WITHOUT A NOTE

Giving anonymously is powerful. Imagine receiving an anonymous gift—it can be from anyone, everyone. And it is. Shhhh.

Ages: Any   *Time:* 30 minutes to gather and deliver

! FUN FACT:

According to a study from the University of Exeter Medical School in England, people who volunteer not only live longer; they also have lower levels of depression, increased life satisfaction, and enhanced well-being.

PRACTICE SPEAKING IN A KIND WAY AND TEACH YOUR CHILDREN TO DO THE SAME

For one day, keep every negative thought, frustration, or complaint to yourself and share only your positive comments with others. And every time you do have a negative thought, counter it out loud with a positive one. Say six nice things to six someones and make their days.

Ages: Any   *Time:* Seconds

CHAPTER SIX

Wacky Times

Musical Family Fun

If music be the food of love, play on.

—WILLIAM SHAKESPEARE

KAZOOS

Put kazoos by your kids' plates at the breakfast table for a zip-a-dee-doo-dah morning.

Ages: 2–5   *Time:* Minutes

MARCHING BAND

Make instruments and turn your family into a marching band. Use some of your toss-away containers like oatmeal containers, coffee cans, or water bottles with beans inside. Grab the wooden spoons and march to the beat of your own drums.

Ages: 2–5   *Time:* 15 minutes to make; 10–20 minutes to march

! *FUN FACT:*

According to the *Journal of Positive Psychology*, researchers at the University of Missouri found listening to music makes you happier. By examining brain scans, scientists found that those who listened to upbeat music experienced a rush of the feel-good neurotransmitter dopamine near the brain's pleasure center.

CRANK UP THE BATH-TIME TUNES

Invest in a waterproof speaker for the bathtub.

Ages: 1–7   *Time:* Varies

GLOW DANCE

Throw a glow-in-the-dark dance party! Get glow sticks, set up black lights, and even douse T-shirts with glow-in-the-dark paint and really trip the night fantastic.

Ages: 3 and up   *Time:* As long as you like!

You're only given a little spark of madness and if you lose that you're nothing.

—ROBIN WILLIAMS

All-Things-Wet-and-Wonderful Fun

WACKY WATER BALLOON WEDNESDAY

Have you ever declared it Wacky Water Balloon Wednesday in your neighborhood? The kids spend the day filling and tying ammunition and then let the water bombs fly.

Ages: All   *Time:* A couple of hours; 1 hour of war

TURN YOUR BACKYARD INTO A WATER PARK

Wacky times await when you turn your backyard into a water park! Buy a blow-up pool. Set up a Slip'N Slide. Turn on the sprinklers. Set up an obstacle course with inner tubes. Turn on the bubble machine!

Ages: 2–7   *Time:* An afternoon of fun

COLORED-WATER FUN

Little kids love indoor water play. Fill lots of clear plastic containers and plastic cups with water, adding drops of fun food coloring to each. Let them pour and mix and match. Mess can be contained if you have them do it by the sink.

Ages: 2–7   *Time:* 1 hour

WALK THE PLANK

Suspend a bridge over a kiddie pool. Use a smooth piece of wood long enough to get children to about the middle of the pool and prop up with bricks. Fill pool with blow-up sharks and plastic fish—or maybe my favorite, an alligator. Make your little pirates walk the plank.

Ages: 2–4   *Time:* Minutes

Dress the Part for Fun

CREATE A DRESS-UP CLOSET

A dress-up closet is a must for little ones. Don't spend a lot, just hoard those old bridesmaid dresses, Halloween costumes, and anything else you can find. Pick up stuff at the thrift store. A full dress-up closet sets the stage for all kinds of creative fun—plays, parades, TV shows, fashion shows, commercial shoots, historical plays, interpretive dance. There is *nothing* the kids can't do when they dress the part.

Ages: All   *Time:* Endless fun

HALLOWEEN PARADE

Why wait for October 31 to host a Halloween parade? Invite the neighbors and have one any time of the year. Costumes are fun to swap and mix up for even goofier looks!

Ages: Any   *Time:* 1 hour

MASKED BALL

It's the finest affair when you turn your house into a masked ball! Stock up on old prom dresses from Goodwill or the local thrift store and cut them down for little girls. Boys will look dapper in bow ties and top hats. Crank up the big band music; you can probably find a collection at your local library—and dance the night away.

Ages: 4–7   *Time:* An evening

CHARACTER DINNER (OR BREAKFAST)

Come to the table dressed as your favorite storybook movie or cartoon character. Pump up the fun by acting in character for the meal. Even serve food your new invented guests might eat, like carrots for *Alice in Wonderland*'s White Rabbit, spinach for Popeye, gummy ants for Arthur, or fancy tea for a Disney princess.

Ages: 3 and up   *Time:* 30 minutes to costume up; mealtime to enjoy

MIXED BAG

Fun and easy to do: keep disguises and costumes in a bag or box. Play musical mix-up. Sit in a circle passing the bag or box around. When the music stops, the person holding the bag closes his or her eyes, reaches inside, and pulls out an item like an oversize pair of sunglasses, clown nose, or long formal gloves. They put on the item and pass the bag along as the music starts up again for another round of fun dress-up. When everyone is good and costumed-up, freeze dance is a great way to keep mixing it up. The group dances to the music. When the music stops, the last person to freeze exchanges a costume item. Or if you want to turn up the competition, toss a pile of dress-up supplies in the middle of the room, divide into two teams, set a timer, and see who can come up with the funniest completed look.

Ages: 4–9   *Time:* 1–2 hours

BIRTHDAY DRESS-UP

Easy-to-make disguises up the fun factor at birthday parties. Cut a simple cape from black felt, securing the top corners with a press-on Velcro tab for a Harry Potter birthday party. Draw on glasses with black eye pencils for a more Harry-ish look. Make crowns for a king or princess party or cat ears for a kitten party. Buy red bandanas for a pirate party.

Ages: 2–6   *Time:* Varies

CHAPTER SEVEN

Bad Times Made Better

Trying Things for the First Time Can Be Scary Unless You Make Them Fun

You gain strength, courage and confidence by every experience in which you really stop to look fear in the face.

—ELEANOR ROOSEVELT

Doing things for the first time can be scary, but if you find a way to make them fun, you forget your fear. I taught my sister, Jen, how to ride a bike in the parking lot behind our apartment when she was four or five. She was scared, and so was I. I kept thinking, *What if she falls and cracks her head?* It was the 1970s, years and years before helmets would become the norm. But I knew she could do it! She would go a bit, but as soon as fear would strike, she was down. "Pretend you are in a parade," I yelled out to her. We were both so small, when the thought of being in a parade was about the most exciting thing you could imagine. Suddenly, I wanted to make Jen *feel* like she was in a parade. I quickly snatched two fistfuls of dandelions and start tossing them in her way, cheering. "You're in a parade! You're in a parade! Look at *you!*" I shouted. Jen smiled wide and biked the whole length of the parking lot, dandelions in her hair. She never looked back—an official two-wheel rider. We still talk about it today. I love how a dose of imaginary F-U-N saved the day and made learning a new skill less scary. Here are a few ideas for banishing fear in favor of fun.

FIRST DAY OF SCHOOL

Invite your child's classmates over for a little lunch before school starts. Buy lots of little school supplies and hide them in the backyard so they can go on a school scavenger hunt, collecting items like erasers, pencils, pens, stickers, and small notebooks in brown paper lunch bags, or surprise them with real lunch bags as a party favor. Such a nice way for the kids to all come together before the first day of school.

Ages: 4–8   *Time:* A couple of hours

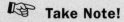 **Take Note!**

For little ones starting school, one of my daughter Ava's favorite books, Rosemary Wells's *Yoko's World of Kindness: Golden Rules for a Happy Classroom,* is a delightful read about Yoko and her kindergarten friends and the challenges and joys of this all-important school year.

DECORATE THEIR LOCKERS

If your little ones have lockers, surprise them by decorating the lockers. There are lots of products on the market to jazz up their space: wallpaper, miniature chandeliers, funky mirrors, magnets, signs, and picture frames for pictures of your family.

Ages: 6–10   *Time:* 20 minutes

Bozzo Family Fun File

Have a nervous little flower girl? Give her a friend. For our wedding, we gave our flower girls Raggedy Ann dolls designed to look like them, complete with matching flower-girl dresses. Custom-designed Raggedy Andy dolls are great for little ring bearers too!

MOVING AWAY FROM FRIENDS

If you are moving away, make stamped envelopes with your child's address on them to hand out at a going-away party. It makes keeping in touch that much easier. A mailbox of letters can make the transition to a new town and school less scary.

Ages: All   *Time:* Varies

Turning Yucky Around

What makes night within us may leave stars.

—Victor Hugo

Sticks and stones and broken bones! There are times when things turn yucky. What to do? Find ways to turn up the fun if you can.

> ### Bozzo Family Fun File
>
> I was frozen when Ava broke her arm when she was six years old. I mean, how do you make *that* fun? My neighbor Freddi B. bought her a monkey T-shirt—the monkey had an arm cast! After that, Ava was so proud of her broken arm. What a way to make her day. I think she wore that shirt every day until her cast came off.

WORRY

We all worry about kids who worry too much. Help them find fun ways to manage their worry, like worry dolls or worry beads. Here is another idea: Grab a Mason jar and a pack of marbles. When they have a worrisome thought, have them whisk it away by putting a marble in the jar. It's helpful for them to transfer their fear and for you to keep track of how much they are worrying so you can make sure there's not a problem.

*The important thing is to teach a child that good can
always triumph over evil.*

—WALT DISNEY

☞ **Take Note!**

Owl Babies by Martin Waddell is great read-along for
little toddlers with big worries.

▼▼▼▼▼▼▼▼▼▼▼▼▼▼▼▼▼▼▼▼▼▼▼▼▼▼▼▼▼▼▼▼▼

Fun from the Field

What do you do when a vacation goes bust? A couple
of years ago Tiffany K.'s family missed their flight to
Florida, with no more flights going out that long President's Day weekend. They stuck to their fun guns and
went on a spontaneous road trip to Galena, Illinois,
instead. They said it was one of the best trips they've
ever taken.

▲▲▲▲▲▲▲▲▲▲▲▲▲▲▲▲▲▲▲▲▲▲▲▲▲▲▲▲▲▲▲▲▲▲

DOROTHY'S TORNADOES, OH MY!

If you want to add a bit of fun to a stormy night, these will
do the trick. Fill a baby food jar three-quarters of the way with
water, adding a few drops of dishwashing liquid. Add a couple
of pinches of glitter and a house from an old Monopoly set.
Quickly spin the jar in a circular motion for a few seconds,
stop, and look inside for a mini tornado forming in the water.
Presto. Tornado on command.

CHAPTER EIGHT

On Your Mark!

Contests and Games

Life is more fun if you play games.   —ROALD DAHL

A MINUTE TO WIN IT

Super fun and super easy. Set players up with tasks to complete in one minute. Tasks should be simple (but hard to do well) using ordinary things from around the house. Grab a stopwatch. Players get three points for trying each task and five points if they finish in a minute. Here are some ideas for tasks to get you started, but feel free to let your imagination run wild:

- Stack twenty-five pennies.
- Put a cookie on your forehead and get it into your mouth using only your facial muscles.
- Transfer twenty-five M&M'S from one plate to another using a straw.

- Put a cereal box that has been cut into pieces back together.
- Stack five apples on top of one another.
- Use a chopstick, string, and a paper clip to go fishing for keys on a key ring.

Ages: 8 and up   *Time:* At least a minute

ROVING GAME OF SCRABBLE

This is a great idea when you have a house full of people and an action-packed holiday weekend or for weeks when everyone is going in their own direction and there is not much time to sit down together for a family game night. Just put the Scrabble game in the corner of a room. When it's your turn, you play a word as you pass through the room, then wait for the next player to take a turn. Keep a running tab, or highest-scoring word of the week wins.

Ages: 8 and up   *Time:* Varies

CUPCAKE WARS

You might be familiar with the hit show *Cake Wars.* In this at-home version, bakers face off and try to make the most creative cupcakes using a wild array of decorations: sprinkles, gumdrops, gels, candied eyeballs, chocolate chips, gummy worms, Smarties, edible flowers, etc. You can buy the cupcakes ready-made or bake them from scratch. Then, ready, set, *decorate*! Post for votes on Facebook or Instagram and declare a winner.

Ages: 6–13   *Time:* An afternoon

BUSY-HANDS PUZZLES

Leave a puzzle on the dining room table, on the kitchen counter, or in a room the kids pass through during the day. Put a few pieces together to give them a start. Soon busy minds with busy fingers will discover it and start adding pieces bit by bit.

Ages: Varies   *Time:* A few minutes (or puzzle pieces); a day until the puzzle is completed

FOR THE BEANS

Fill a jar with jelly beans, Skittles, gumballs, even pennies (don't forget to count them), and leave out slips for everyone to guess how many are in the jar. Set it out on the breakfast table and announce the winner at dinner. Closest number wins.

Ages: 3–7 *Time:* About 15 minutes to count and fill the jar; seconds to guess

THE AMAZING RACE

Turn an ordinary day or even a birthday into *The Amazing Race.* Teams travel in a group with a phone or digital camera. Like the TV show, you send the kids out with clues and challenges to solve and act out before the other team. Before you begin, tell each team that the goal is to figure out where to go, take a photograph in that location, and then text each picture to the game runner (usually a parent). Each team is allowed two lifeline calls. Place the tasks in sealed envelopes numbered in order, staggering the tasks between the two teams so that they don't show up at the same place at the same time. Teams read the clue, orchestrate the picture, then open the next clue quickly to stay ahead of the other team. Teams are judged on how many clues they've solved and the creativity of their pictures. The big fun is putting all the pictures and videos in a slideshow to play later in the evening.

Ages: 11 and up   *Time:* A day for setup; 90 minutes to solve

NEIGHBORHOOD SCAVENGER HUNT

Send the kids out into the neighborhood on a scavenger hunt. Each team gets a list of ordinary household items you have to "borrow" from a neighbor—a can of corn, sunglasses, a Christmas ornament. First group home with the goods wins.

Ages: 8 and up   *Time:* 1–2 hours

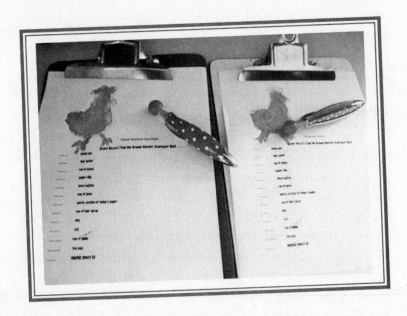

Bozzo Family Fun File

One year I surprised the kids with a live rooster as one of the finds on a scavenger hunt. I had borrowed one just for the day from a live poultry store and hid it at my friend Tessa E.'s house. It was the one item the kids thought they'd never find in our sleepy little suburban town. It was a scavenger hunt no one will forget!

COLD WARS: HAVE A SNOWMAN CONTEST

On your mark, get set—which team can build an entire snowman first?

Ages: 3–10   *Time:* 30 minutes

Let the Games Begin!

Childhood is a short season.   —HELEN HAYES

The Olympics only come around every two years, so why not make them F-U-N!

TABLETOP CURLING

You don't need a big space to try your hand at curling. Try tabletop curling. Buy a big piece of poster board and make a bull's-eye at one end using construction paper or markers. Grab a handful of bottle caps and put a sticker on each to keep tabs on players, then flick the caps toward the bull's-eye with your fingers. Score as usual.

Ages: 5–13   *Time:* 30 minutes

HOCKEY FEVER

Grab some brooms and catch a little hockey fever with broomball. You can play anywhere, and ice is optional.

Ages: 5–13   *Time:* 20 minutes

Turning Your Home into Fitness Fun

BACKYARD YOGA

Try some backyard yoga with the kids or the neighbors. Meet up in the morning (maybe for the sunrise?) and namaste the day.

Ages: Any   *Time:* Varies

OBSTACLE COURSE

Gather some old tires and build an obstacle course in the backyard.

Ages: 5–15   *Time:* 1 hour

LET'S GET PHYSICAL

Create an exercise video together and then work out to it as a family.

Ages: Any   *Time:* Varies

CHAPTER NINE

Green Fun

Planting Your Own Fun

WILDFLOWERS

Pick wildflowers together in an open field. It's a great thing to do on your way to a party or backyard tea. Fresh wildflowers make the ultimate hostess gift and nothing can be more simple and memorable than spending time in the sun collecting bouquets. Tie your finds with ribbon or twine. Not headed anywhere? Leave the flowers in a Mason jar on an elderly neighbor's porch or at the local nursing home.

Ages: 2–8   *Time:* Minutes or longer

GO FISHING

Remember fishing? So fun! And easy to do if you can find a park with a stocked pond where a naturalist will loan you a fishing pole, help you bait those hooks, and help you release the fish you catch.

Ages: 2–13   *Time:* A fun morning or afternoon

BIT OF HONEY

Bees! It's so fun to watch them at work; they are so B-U-S-Y. Many nature centers have beehives set up for viewing; even some restaurants and hotels where they collect natural honey for their recipes keep hives. Totally worth the time to observe these fascinating insects. Trust me—it's the bee's knees.

Ages: Any   *Time:* A fun half afternoon

CALLING ALL WEATHER GIRLS AND BOYS!

Set up a weather station in your backyard. Kids will have lots of fun measuring rainfall in a tall jar or vase (just dip a ruler inside to measure). You can even make it super fancy with a beaker. Hang an outdoor thermometer and make a homemade anemometer to measure wind. It's easy to make. Just poke four equally spaced holes in a Dixie cup and insert two straws to form an X, threading them through, crossing one over the other. Add a pencil-sized hole at the bottom of the cup. Insert a pencil into that bottom hole so that the eraser is up against the X of the straws. Push a pushpin through the other side of the X of the straws and into the pencil eraser to secure. Cut two equal holes on opposite sides of four other Dixie cups and thread one cup through each straw end horizontally, positioning the cups so that the opening of one cup faces the bottom of the one before it. Mark your lead cup, and count the rotations. Ten turns in one minute is equal to one mile per hour of wind speed.

Ages: 6 and up   *Time:* 40 minutes

READY, SET, WEATHER ACTION

Put those weather findings to good use by making your own weather report. You can buy a green screen for about $50, or you can make your own by painting a wall in your garage or basement bright green or by hanging a bright green sheet or other piece of fabric. Have your little weatherman or weatherwoman prepare and memorize their weather report. Position them three feet in front of the green screen. Make sure to put a light off to the side so there is no shadow on the background. Then import your video and edit your weather report using video-editing software such as Adobe Premiere or Microsoft Movie Maker.

Ages: 8–13   *Time:* A couple of days

PLANT PUMPKINS FOR HALLOWEEN!

Why not plan on growing your own Halloween pumpkins this year? Pick up some pumpkin seeds and plant three to five of them about an inch apart. Once they begin to germinate, thin out your crop, leaving just the healthiest. If you live in the North, look to get those pumpkins planted in mid- to late May. If you are in a southern climate, think June.

Ages: All   *Time:* Minutes to plant

FOR THE BIRDS?

Encourage a little nesting in your backyard by creating a nesting basket to put outdoors for birds to use to build their nests. Use any old basket, filling it with materials birds can use to build their nests, like cloth strips, string, ribbons, tiny twigs, animal hair, moss, and feathers.

Ages: 3–13   *Time:* An afternoon

☞ **Take Note!**

After helping mother birds build nests for their baby birds, your little bird might enjoy a lap-side reading of the beautiful book *Are You My Mother?* or *The Best Nest* by P. D. Eastman.

Create Treasure with Upcycled Art Projects

SCRABBLE PLAQUE

Take old Scrabble tiles and spell out words that describe those you love—"top pop," "awesome grandma," "you are great"—then glue in a shadow box or frame for a great gift.

Ages: 3–10   *Time:* 30 minutes

PHOTO PHOTOSYNTHESIS

Tape pictures on pencils, wooden sticks, or chopsticks. Fill a flowerpot with rice or floral foam and plant for a fun decoration.

Ages: 3–10   *Time:* 15 minutes

RAINY-DAY PLANTERS

Take little rubber boots the toddlers have outgrown and plant little plants in them.

Ages: 3–10   *Time:* Minutes

Bozzo Family Fun File

My girls loved making their own purses out of jeans. My aunt used to make these with me and my cousins. Cut the legs off of a pair of jeans. Turn the jeans inside out. Sew the two leg openings closed and cut a strap from the leftover leg material. Sew on the strap and add fun patches and trims to your "brand-new" purse.

COFFEE CUP SLEEVES

Make cute coffee cup sleeves. Cut an old headband and place around a cup, securing it with a safety pin or stapling the ends. Decorate with stick-on rhinestones or even an old baby hair bow.

Ages: 3–10   *Time:* 30 minutes

FISHY FISH

Cut the bottom off an old two-liter bottle. Staple the end to create a fin, and use the top as a fishy mouth. Add a wiggle eye, and then paint your fish tropical colors.

Ages: 3–8   *Time:* 45 minutes

TIN CAN ROBOTS

Don't can those old tin cans. There are lots of ways to make a tin can robot! Start with clean cans, then line the inside seam with duct or electrical tape to keep little fingers safe. Gather milk jug lids, shower rings, pieces of zigzag ribbon, pipe cleaners, Ping-

Pong balls, Christmas garland, wiggle eyes, and buttons to glue onto the can for fun robot features. Use Elmer's glue or hot glue.

Ages: 3–5   *Time:* 30 minutes

LP PENGUINS

If you have old albums and no way to play them, they make terrific penguin wings. Cut an old record in half and adhere each half to the side of a shoe box painted black, glue white craft fur on the chest, and attach a small box for the head. Finish with eyes and a beak.

Ages: 3–8   *Time:* 30 minutes

ALLEY ALLIGATORS

Turn an egg carton or packing carton into a friendly alligator. Cut the carton in half, cutting the back seam and dislodging the top from the bottom. Paint the inside red and the outside green. Glue Popsicle sticks painted white to the alligator's mouth—the more crooked the better. Glue on Ping-Pong ball eyeballs. Hinge the top to the bottom by clipping the back with binder clips. Argh!

Ages: 3–5   *Time:* 30 minutes

OWL BOOK HOLDER

Glue an old record album onto each side of a large wooden wine box for owl wings. Paint the box and albums brown. Add eyes and a beak with foam paper. Keep books inside for those little night-owl readers.

Ages: 8–10   *Time:* 45 minutes

Grunge Fun

When it comes to fun, get down and dirty.

Of all the paths you take in life, make sure a few of them are dirt.

—JOHN MUIR

MAKE MUD PIES TOGETHER

Such classic play! Even set up a mud pie kitchen with a toy kitchen set! Take an old toy kitchen set and lots of old bowls for mud mixing, old cake pans for pretend mud-pie baking, even old plastic cups for pretend mudslide shakes.

Ages: 2–5   *Time:* 30 minutes

MAKE MUD BRICKS

Mix mud and water and pour the soupy mess into ice cube trays. Let them dry in the sun for a couple of days and pop them out for fantastic, fun, creative play. For bigger bricks, try using rectangular plastic bins you use for storage.

Ages: 2–5   *Time:* 30 minutes to make; a couple of days to dry

DIG FOR DINOSAUR BONES

Calling all paleontologists! Make your own bones with salt clay dough or buy plastic bones. Bury them in the yard, and set your little dino diggers to work. Don't forget goggles, chisels, shovels, brushes, and a notepad for recording findings. If the weather forces you inside, fill a baby pool with shredded newspaper or even tire material and hide the bones for fun finding.

Ages: 2–6   *Time:* 30 minutes

MAKE A VOLCANO

Make a volcano out of mud. Let it dry, then add baking soda, red food coloring, and vinegar for the eruption.

Ages: 4–8   *Time:* 1 hour, including drying time

CHAPTER TEN

Lots of Fun for Little and Big Ones

End-of-the-Day Fun

It was only a sunny smile, and little it cost in the giving, but like morning light it scattered the night and made the day worth living.

—F. Scott Fitzgerald

FLASHLIGHT HIDE-AND-SEEK

Turn off all the lights and challenge the kids to a game of flashlight hide-and-seek.

Ages: 2–7 *Time:* 15 magical minutes

FLASHLIGHT PAJAMA WALK

Go on a flashlight pajama walk around the block. Little imaginations loom large at night when it's quiet and the earth's "lights" are off. Ask them to look for tree frogs, bats, and other nocturnal creatures.

Ages: 2–8   *Time:* 15 magical minutes

NIGHTTIME CRITTER HUNT

Take the above idea a step further. Take the kids on a nighttime critter hunt in a nearby wooded area. We borrowed this idea from our favorite family destination, Horseshoe Canyon Ranch in Jasper, Arkansas, where the wranglers lead all the little ones on a critter hunt while the grown-ups go on a moonlight horseback ride. Don't worry, it's not a *hunt* but rather a critter *find.* You don't have to find much—even an itsy-bitsy spider gives them the giggles and sends shivers up their spines. Forehead lights required.

Ages: 1–5   *Time:* A few minutes to half an hour

DRAW THE NIGHT SKY

At dusk, gather the kids, a blanket, clipboards, black construction paper, and chalk or white crayons and head for a patch of earth where the stars shine bright at night, maybe a park or a neighborhood golf course. If you have a constellations book or want to check one out at the library, it's great to bring along or study beforehand. Or maybe just do a quick Google search of popular stars to spot. Lie on your back and draw the night sky together, identifying constellations as you go. Simple starry pictures are fun too. And keep the magic going when you get home. Pick up a set of glow-in-the-dark ceiling stars and have the kids re-create the constellations they discovered on their bedroom ceiling. They will remember this fun little evening for a long time.

Ages: 3–8   *Time:* 40 magical minutes

CATCH LIGHTNING BUGS

Gather some jelly jars, remove the circle part of the lids, and replace with a piece of tulle held on with a rubber band. Add a moist paper towel to the bottom of the jar. Come darkness, let the firefly frenzy begin. Catch with a net or by gently cupping your hands around them. Be sure to release the bugs when you are done. The folks at the Smithsonian suggest a release no longer than a day or two after capture.

Ages: 4 and up   *Time:* 20 minutes

TENT AND STORY TIME

On busy nights with lots of reading still to be done, make a blanketed tent in the living room and invite everyone to climb inside for a good old-fashioned family book night. If needed, add a lamp for a reading light. Battery-operated candles or flashlights make it fun.

Ages: 4–9   *Time:* 30 minutes

SEW ON!

For the crafty set, let the kids try their hand at sewing—by hand or machine. Cut a simple shape out of fuzzy material and make your own stuffed animal with button eyes and a pom-pom nose. Or make a sleeveless nightgown. Or for a super-duper simple starter, a pillow.

Ages: 6–11   *Time:* 1–2 hours

NIGHT-LIGHTS

Make your own night-light with a Mason jar (without the lid) and a tea light. Fun to decorate with adhesive rhinestones and stickers. If the candle makes you wary, there are many battery-operated candles on the market, like Playbulb.

Ages: 4–8   *Time:* 45 minutes

DOWN UNDER

Have the kids sleep under their beds—it's fun to set up their little secret spot!

Ages: 3–5   *Time:* A fun night

LET OUT LANTERNS IN THE NIGHT SKY

Salute a special day spent together by launching sky lanterns just before bedtime.

Ages: Any   *Time:* 20 minutes

! **FUN FACT:**

Did you know? The traditional bedtime story is dying. According to a study by Littlewoods.com, 91 percent of parents said they were regularly read stories as children, yet today, the average child hears only three bedtime stories a week.

GLOW-IN-THE-DARK BOWLING

Turn your driveway into a glow bowl with two-liter bottles filled with water and glow sticks—simply drop the sticks in to make the glow go. Arrange in bowling-pin formation. Then grab a slightly deflated basketball or an old medicine ball (dipped in glow-in-the-dark paint and dried beforehand) and *strike*.

Ages: 1 to 5   *Time:* A few minutes to half an hour

A MOONLIGHT ESCAPE

There is a terrific scene in the old movie *Stepmom* with Susan Sarandon and Julia Roberts. The mom wakes her teenager in the middle of the night and takes her on a snowy, surprise horseback ride. Such a beautiful moment between mom and daughter. One night, find a way to create a moonlight escape of your own—could be a slow drive or just a picnic blanket and the first glimpse of the sunrise.

Ages: Teens   *Time:* 30 minutes–1 hour

Bozzo Family Fun File

Going to the Mattresses

Nights when my husband would travel, the girls and I would have a secret plan.

At night, we'd go to the mattresses. I'd pull the girls' mattresses off their beds (mine too!) and put them in front of the fireplace. It's so fun and easy to do. We loved it being our little secret (Dad likes things neat), but there's no reason now to keep this great idea to ourselves. They loved setting up their "camp" with favorite stuffed animals, books to read, and pj's for the night. We'd roast hot dogs in the fireplace for dinner and marshmallows for dessert, read stories, and giggle as we all fell asleep together.

Ages: 4–8   **Time:** All evening and night

SLEEP-UNDER

What's a sleep-under? It's a nighttime pajama party for kids not quite old enough for a sleepover. We'd invite the little neighbors over in their fluffy pajamas, have pizza, do a craft, and watch a movie or read books before everyone went home and turned in for the night in their own bed. Swap nights with your neighbors and give the moms and dads a chance to steal away for a Friday night dinner for two.

Ages: 4 and up   **Time:** 3 hours

GLOW-IN-THE-DARK RING TOSS

Fill two-liter bottles with water and drop in glow sticks—just pop them in whole. Line up and toss shower rings, trying to land them around the necks of the bottles.

Ages: 4 and up   *Time:* 15–30 minutes

DRIVEWAY DRIVE-IN

Turn your garage door into a drive-in movie. It's easy to do with a pocket-sized projector; Brookstone makes a nice one you can hook up to your phone or laptop to stream your favorite flick. Grab the lawn chairs, lots of blankets, and popcorn, of course. Even set up a candy counter using a cardboard box for a drive-in concession stand. And don't forget the bug spray.

Ages: 4 and up   *Time:* 3 hours

☞ Take Note!

You can turn the Driveway Drive-in idea into a great at-home birthday party. The kids can even sleep in a tent in the backyard.

BATHTUB MESS-TERPIECES

Squirt shaving cream in a plastic bowl and add color with Color Fizzers True Color Tablets (which won't stain like food coloring) and paintbrushes. Let the kids *paint* themselves clean.

Ages: 2 and up   *Time:* Until they start to shrivel

MR. BUBBLE

Invest in a bubble machine and aim it toward the tub at bath time for added nighttime pop.

Ages: 2 and up   *Time:* Until they start to shrivel

HOWL AT THE MOON

Lots of energy before bed? Let the dogs out to howl at the moon. Fun if they wear fluffy brown or black footie pajamas. Vanilla wafers make a good "dog treat."

Ages: 2–4   *Time:* Seconds

PORCH-LIGHT BITES

Have a bedtime snack by candlelight on the front porch.

Ages: 2 and up   *Time:* 5 minutes

PLAY HIDE AND SLEEP

A great little game for toddlers who don't like bedtime. Hide all the items your child needs for bed—toothbrush, toothpaste, pajamas, bedtime doll or stuffed animal, and bedtime story. They have to do the task associated with each item found: put on pajamas when they find them, brush teeth when they find their toothbrush, and sit for a story when they find their bedtime book. You'll have them ready for bed without squabbling.

Ages: 2–3   *Time:* 15–30 minutes

☞ **Take Note!**

A good little read for little ones who can't get to sleep? *Bedtime for Frances* by Russell Hoban.

HAVE A PILLOW FIGHT

After all, what are pillows for?

Ages: All   *Time:* 5 minutes

TURN ON THE NIGHTLY NEWS

Challenge your child to be a newscaster giving you a news report of their day's happenings in their best broadcasting voice. A thumb makes a quick and efficient microphone. A cute way for quiet ones to share their day with you.

Ages: 7–9   *Time:* 5 minutes

THROW A FULL-MOON PARTY!

Next time there is a full moon—or even better, a blue moon—celebrate with the kids before hiking out to moon-bathe. On the menu? MoonPies, Pop Rocks, crescent rolls, Swiss cheese. Wear red to honor the moon goddesses like Isis and Diana. Make moon crafts. One simple way? Cut a white paper plate into a half-moon shape and finish off with its face. Or let them paint a moon on black paper with white paint and flour for fun textured craters. Or make moons with salt dough clay or papier-

! FUN FACT:

Did you know it's a Chinese custom to make moon food, including moon cakes—round cakes made of flour and brown sugar stuffed with sweets—to celebrate the Moon Festival? On the night of the full moon between early September and early October, they also celebrate by gazing at the moon and making colorful lanterns.

mâché. Finish off with the beloved book *Goodnight Moon* by Margaret Wise Brown.

Ages: 2 and up   *Time:* 1 hour

Pint-Sized Fun

BOOM!

Pull out pots and pans and wooden spoons and let them go to town.

Ages: Baby   *Time:* 30 minutes

TENT FUN

Put up a bed tent on your little one's bed. Makes bedtime mysterious and fun.

Ages: 3–6   *Time:* Lots of magical evenings

CREATIVE CASTLES

Build a fairy or a king's castle out of an old refrigerator box—appliance stores are always happy to donate. Three refrigerator boxes and a dryer box will build the perfect kingdom. Just fold for transporting, then reassemble at home. Cut doors and windows with a box cutter—you can add a little castle trim and turrets if you are super handy. Paint with a thick house paint. Let dry and have fun!

Ages: 3–8   *Time:* A weekend to build, paint, and decorate; play until it collapses

SHUT THE FRONT DOOR

Let them color your front door with Crayola washable paint for hands-on holiday decoration.

Ages: 3–5   *Time:* 20 minutes

PLAY WITH DOUGH

Make homemade Play-Doh. Nothing is more wholesome when it comes to fun, and you don't have to worry if they eat it! Mix two cups of flour, one cup of water, two tablespoons of vegetable oil, a few drops of food coloring, and one table-spoon of cream of tartar, and stir constantly over low heat. As the dough begins to pull away from the sides of the pan, re-move from the heat and allow to cool, then knead.

Ages: 1–4   *Time:* 15 minutes to make; 30 minutes of play

BUTTERFLIES

Grab a butterfly net and take the kids on a butterfly chase.

Ages: 3–5   *Time:* 30 minutes

NATURE WALK

Go on a nature walk through the woods.

Ages: 3–10   *Time:* 1 hour

LAUNDRY BASKET CARS

Rev up your laundry basket with a pillow and a plastic plate for a steering wheel and let 'em start those engines—one pushes, one drives.

Ages: 2–3   *Time:* 20 minutes

CARDBOARD BOX TRAIN

Turn an old cardboard box into your little one's favorite choo-choo train with paint, markers, and construction paper.

Ages: 1–3   *Time:* 20 minutes

WATER TAXI

If there is a water taxi in your town, take it. To little ones, it's like a cruise ship.

Ages: 2–9   **Time:** 5–10 minutes

TURKEY CARDS

What to do with those little feet and hands? All you need is a plain piece of card stock, fabric paint, a red balloon, and two wiggle eyes. Dip a hand in paint and press it onto the card stock for the turkey body. You can paint fingers bright colors and use brown for the body. Decorate your turkey with a couple wiggle eyes and a red balloon for the wattle.

Ages: Infant–10   **Time:** 20–30 minutes

▼▼▼▼▼▼▼▼▼▼▼▼▼▼▼▼▼▼▼▼▼▼▼▼▼▼▼▼▼▼▼▼▼▼

Fun from the Field

Worried about mess or, worse, little hands in little mouths? Sarah D. finger-paints with her baby Evie with a Ziploc bag. It's a great way to do it. Just put a piece of paper inside a large Ziploc bag, plop bits of finger paint on the paper, then seal. Baby smears the paint from outside the bag. All the fun with no mess.

▲▲▲▲▲▲▲▲▲▲▲▲▲▲▲▲▲▲▲▲▲▲▲▲▲▲▲▲▲▲▲▲▲▲

RUDOLPH CARDS

Same idea as the turkey cards, only use baby's foot for the reindeer's head; toes make the cutest antlers. Add a red pom-pom for the nose and two wiggle eyes.

Ages: Baby   *Time:* 20–30 minutes

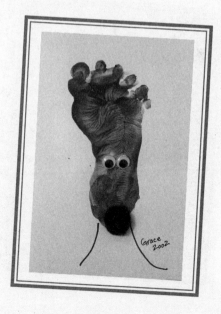

Fun for the Eye-Rolling Teens

GET THE MEMO!

Wish we would have done this years ago! I recently hung up a whiteboard in our mudroom and it's been such a big hit. I thought it would mainly be used for reminders and "be home at 6:00"–type notes, but it's become a fun board with good-luck messages, funny jokes, and welcomes to visiting friends. If you prefer, use the fridge as a memo board or paint a wall or a portion of the wall with chalkboard paint. Happy-colored chalk is a must.

Ages: All   *Time:* Seconds to write; seconds to read!

FACETIME FUN

Have fun with FaceTime good-night calls—a good *call* as teens start to go to bed at different times and the house seems to scatter a bit with different homework schedules. Although you may miss the moonlit tuck-in time just before bedtime, a funny FaceTime chat can be a hoot. Find creative ways to say good night, whether it's a song or a good-night message delivered in a foreign language—or even delivered by a favorite stuffed animal.

Ages: Teens   *Time:* Seconds

HAVE YOUR SELFIE A VERY MERRY TIME!

Selfies are like the new family fun. It's your hilarious signature on a day spent together. Take family selfies whenever you can—even save up that best shot for this year's holiday card: *Have Yourselfie a Very Merry Christmas!*

Ages: Teens   *Time:* Seconds

CHAPTER ELEVEN

Fun That Teaches

Business 101 Fun

Encourage your kids to pretend to be little businesspeople and find ways to make a little (or a lot) of money for FUN!

GATORADE, ANYONE?

If you live by a high school football field where there are sweaty players coming off the field, set up a Gatorade stand.

Ages: 6–15   *Time:* A couple of hours

PLAN A CARNIVAL IN THE BACKYARD

Set up a mini carnival in your backyard—smart idea for teens looking to make a little money while having a lot of fun with the kiddos in the neighborhood. Outgrown stuffed animals get a second life as prizes. Here are a few ideas for carnival games to give you inspiration.

Ages: 10–15   *Time:* A day to set up; a day to carnival

▼▼▼▼▼▼▼▼▼▼▼▼▼▼▼▼▼▼▼▼▼▼▼▼▼▼▼▼▼▼▼▼▼▼

Fun from the Field

Drowning in too much stuff and looking for a way to entertain your teen plus teach them a little bit about earning money? My neighbors had way too much stuff after they built and decorated their new home. Instead of giving all the old décor away, my neighbor challenged her teenage daughter to sell the goods online for 50 percent of whatever she sold. Smart mama!

▲▲▲▲▲▲▲▲▲▲▲▲▲▲▲▲▲▲▲▲▲▲▲▲▲▲▲▲▲▲▲▲▲▲

Tin Can Toss

A classic carnival game made from recycled metal cans. Spray paint cans in bright colors, covering sharp edges with duct tape. Stack on a table—players try to knock all the cans down by throwing a baseball (or Wiffle ball) at the stack.

Duck Game

Fill a baby pool with water and put rubber ducks inside. Beforehand, write the types of prizes your winners will win on the bottom of the rubber duck—so maybe small, medium, and large if your prizes range in three sizes, or red, white, and blue—instructing winners to pull a prize from a red basket, white basket, or blue basket. The great thing about this game? Everyone's a winner.

Ring Toss

Assemble glass Coke bottles in a wooden box close together. Players try to ring a bottle with a shower curtain ring.

Ping-Pong Throw

Arrange empty Pringles cans, lids off, in the shape of a square or triangle. Tape the cans together with duct tape so they don't topple over. Players fling Ping-Pong balls, trying to get them into the cans.

Dart Balloons

Blow up balloons and arrange on a bulletin board. Players throw darts for the pop.

Face-Painting and Tattoo Station

Little kids love these!

Science Fun!

Encouraging learning at home is the number-one thing you can do to ensure academic success, but it doesn't have to be a chore. The following experiments are sure to have future scientists loving learning.

RUBBER EGG

Put a raw egg into a drinking glass and cover it with vinegar. The next day pour out the vinegar, rinse the egg, and refill the glass with vinegar. Leave for six days in its first refresh of vinegar. When it's done, you'll have a rubber bouncy egg! Don't worry, it doesn't smell. It's actually pickled. Try bouncing it (gently) in the sink because it will eventually burst.

What the Fun?!

Here's What Happened: Vinegar is a weak acid. Eggshell is made of calcium carbonate. When the two come together they create a chemical reaction that breaks down the calcium carbonate and produces carbon dioxide. Eventually the shell dissolves and you are left with a rubbery, translucent egg. Pretty cool.

Ages: 3–8   *Time:* 1 week

BENDY BONES

Same concept. Same fun. Soak a chicken bone—a leg bone works great—in vinegar for three days. Take it out and you have a bendy bone.

What the Fun?!

Here's What Happened: Again, vinegar, being a mild acid, dissolves the bone's calcium, and once the calcium is dissolved, there is nothing left to keep it hard.

Ages: 3–8   *Time:* 1 week

HEALTH NOTE

Tell the kids that is why you are always telling them to drink milk! The calcium in milk goes to our bones to make them stronger.

SLIME

Gooey-ooey fun that never gets old. Mix half a cup of Elmer's glue with half a cup of water. Add fun food coloring if you like. In another bowl, mix one teaspoon of Borax with one cup of water until the Borax is dissolved. Add the glue

mixture to the Borax solution, stirring slowly. Slime begins to form immediately; stir for as long as you can, then knead it with your hands. Store in a plastic bag in the fridge to keep it from getting moldy.

What the Fun?!

Here's What Happened: The Borax combines the glue molecules. As they combine, they get gluier—resulting in a thicker, stretchier glue, sssslllliimmme!

Ages: 3–8   *Time:* A few minutes to make; lots of time for fun

RAISE BUTTERFLIES

Raise caterpillars into butterflies with a butterfly larvae kit. The kids will get such a kick out of watching the magical metamorphosis and get a fantastic science education without even knowing it is anything other than fun. Order online and the kit comes right to your home with everything you need.

Ages: 5–10   *Time:* About 4 weeks

☞ **Take Note!**

Two things to make butterfly raising even more fun! Make a caterpillar out of an egg carton. Remove the lid from the egg carton. Cut the bottom portion in half lengthwise down the middle so you have a row of egg holders for the caterpillar's body. Paint the body, either making each egg compartment a different color or using all one color. Add wiggle eyes to the face and draw a smile or glue a piece of red yarn in the shape of a smile. Poke two pieces of pipe cleaner into the caterpillar's head and wrap the top end of each pipe cleaner around a mini pom-pom to make fun and funky antennae. Then make the caterpillar into a butterfly using two wire hangers, some pipe cleaners, glue, tissue paper, glitter, and paint. Bend the hooks of both hangers, collapsing them flat. Attach your hanger-wire wings by securing them with pipe cleaners, wrapping the pipe cleaner around and around the wings until they are attached. Then lightly cover the edges with glue and two sheets of tissue paper. Trim and decorate with watercolor paints, markers, and glitter. And don't forget to read one of our family favorites, the wonderful *The Very Hungry Caterpillar* by Eric Carle.

RAISE TADPOLES

Raise tadpoles into frogs. eBay is a good place to get them. Even better—share your batch with the neighbor kids and raise frogs together this summer.

Ages: 3–12   *Time:* 6–9 weeks

☞ Take Note!

It's so fun to make a frog friend. Cut out a frog shape on two sheets of green felt or material. Mom hot-glues or sews the edges of the body together, leaving a small opening. Kids fill with beans or rice. Glue or sew the hole, then add eyes and a red felt tongue! Then leapfrog into a great read—*Frog and Toad Are Friends* by Arnold Lobel.

MAKE ROCK CANDY

A sweet science treat, rock candy is easy to make and fun to eat. You'll need string or a wooden skewer (a chopstick works just fine), a tall glass, a clothespin, three cups of sugar, and one cup of water. Boil the water in a pan, adding the sugar about a quarter cup at a time, stirring constantly, then adding more as the sugar dissolves. Remove the sugar solution from the heat and let cool. Add food coloring for fun color. Once it's cooled, pour into the bottom of the tall glass. Dip the skewer or string in the sugar solution, roll in about a tablespoon of sugar, then attach the clothespin at the top of it, perpendicular to the skewer or string. Let the skewer or string hang down into the middle of the glass, with the end about an inch from the bottom, by allowing the attached clothespin to balance across the top of the glass. In a few days, the sugar crystals will start to form on the skewer or string, creeping up as they grow.

What the Fun?!

Here's What Happened: You supersaturated the water with sugar by heating it—it took in more sugar than it can hold when it's not hot. As the water cools, the sugar crystals need to cling to something so they start to grow on the skewers or string.

Ages: 3–12 (with adult help at the stove)   *Time:* About 1 week

HOMEMADE LAVA LAMP

A lamp that bobs with wavy globs is so groovy, and easy to make. Just grab a clean one-liter soda bottle and add three-quarters of a cup of water, then fill the rest of the bottle with vegetable oil. Add a few drops of food coloring and half an Alka-Seltzer tablet. Put on the lid and watch the groovy-moovy fun begin. For added fun, shine a flashlight on the bottle.

What the Fun?!

Here's What Happened: The oil stays above the water because oil is lighter (or less dense) than water. Oil and water do not mix because of intermolecular polarity—meaning water molecules (or drops) are like magnets that are attracted to one another (molecular polarity). The same with the oil drops—they are only attracted to one another. When you add the Alka-Seltzer tablet, the gas bubbles rise to the top, taking some of the colored water with them. When the gas escapes at the top, the water dips back down to the bottom. Add another half tablet any time you want to recharge your lava lamp.

Ages: 4–10   *Time:* 15 minutes

BALLOON BLOWOUT

How do you blow up a balloon without, well, blowing it up? With science. Add an inch of warm water to a small, clean soda bottle. Pour in a packet of yeast; swirl it around. Then add a teaspoon of sugar, swirling again. Blow up and deflate a balloon a few times to loosen it, then stretch it over the neck of the bottle. Let the bottle sit in a warm spot for about fifteen minutes and watch the balloon inflate.

What the Fun?!

Here's What Happened: Yeast is actually living—so tiny you can't see them—hungry little microorganisms. As the yeast eats the sugar, it releases a gas called carbon dioxide, which fills the bottle and eventually the balloon as more gas is created.

Ages: 3–6   *Time:* 30 minutes

MAKE SODA BOTTLE TERRARIUMS

A terrarium is a fun way to teach kids about the water cycle, and it's easy to make one with an old two-liter soda bottle. Cut off the top about four inches down and cover the bottom of the bottle with small stones about half an inch deep to provide drainage. They will allow extra water to flow to the bottom, preventing the soil on top of the stones from getting too muddy. Fill the bottle halfway with potting soil and add small, slow-growing plants like African violets, jade, small ferns, or a spider plant. You can substitute seeds, but make sure that they are for small plants. Then tape the top of the bottle back on, with the lid screwed on, and place on a windowsill that gets indirect sunlight. Too much sun will evaporate the natural water and scorch the plants. Keep an eye on your terrarium for a few days to make sure it has the right moisture level. Look for water droplets on the sides and top. If you don't see any, add a bit of water. If there is too much water on the sides and top, remove the lid for a few hours to let some of it evaporate. After you find a balance, the terrarium will continue to maintain its own eco-balance.

What the Fun?!

Here's What Happened: You created a miniature world. And here's how it works: the plant leaves release water vapor, which condenses on the soda bottle, trickles down into the dirt, and re-waters the plants, all in a cycle that doesn't need to be supplemented if the container is airtight.

Ages: 5–12   *Time:* 1 week

A CLOSED AQUATIC ECOSYSTEM

Take a Mason jar with a lid and, using a funnel, add mud you've scooped from a pond. If you prefer to skip that step, you can purchase substrate at the store. Add algae from a pond or a small plant you purchase, such as pond weed or willow moss. Add a layer of sand, being careful not to crush the plants, then add a layer of either gravel taken from a pond or aquatic gravel from the store. Add pond, aquarium, or unfiltered water you've let sit out for twenty-four to seventy-two hours. Fill only three-quarters of the way to leave room for air. Choose two algae-eating animals for your ecosystem, like cherry shrimp or Malaysian snails. Don't buy more than two for one ecosystem. There will be too many to survive. Before adding them, let them acclimate to the water temperature by floating the plastic bag they are in on the surface of the water for a few hours. Then add them. Keep your ecosystem near a window, but not one that gets direct sunlight. Shrimp and snails need to be in a place where the temperature is between 68 and 82 degrees Fahrenheit. For more exotic sea animals like starfish and sea anemones, you can make your ecosystem a saltwater system by replacing freshwater plants with marine plants such as *Caulerpa* algae or bubble algae. Watch your system for the first few days to make sure you have the right balance. If your plants look unhealthy or your water is cloudy, try more sunlight. If your plants or fish start to die, move to a spot with less sunlight. If your plants become too big, add shrimp or snails. If you would like to save time, you can buy everything you need (except water) to build an ecosystem or even buy your own already-put-together ecosystem from Eco-Sphere.com or Amazon.com.

What the Fun?!

Here's What Happened: By creating a closed ecosystem, you've created a tiny working model of Earth by assembling the same essential elements found on our planet: air, water, life. The sea life lives by consuming algae and breathing oxygen from the water. Its waste is broken down by bacteria and converted to carbon dioxide to feed the algae. The algae use light to convert the carbon dioxide into oxygen for the sea life to breathe. All the inhabitants provide for one another to sustain a living environment. Nothing goes to waste in a balanced ecosystem.

Ages: 5–12   *Time:* 1 week

SCIENCE LAB

Set up a science lab in the crummiest corner of your basement. It's not hard or expensive. You can find cheap beakers

and lab flasks online. Goggles and lab coats make it feel official. Stock the lab with easy-to-buy materials like baking soda
and vinegar—it's so exciting to make a bubbly concoction
while learning about carbon dioxide gas. Magnets are great
for teaching about magnetic fields and electromagnetism. A
double scale shows a preschooler that a handful of stones
weighs more than a scoop of flour. Packets of seeds, a bag of
soil, a spoon, and an egg carton give little ones what they need
to grow their own garden. A pile of dull pennies shines up fast
in a bowl of vinegar—the acid in the vinegar removes the cop-
per oxide that's crusted on the pennies.

Ages: All   *Time:* Ongoing

Reading Fun

FAMILY BOOK CLUB

Make reading fun for kids by starting a family book club.
Celebrate the finish with a book party with fun activities that
pair the book's theme and characters. So maybe that means a
special lunch at the local conservatory if you read *The Secret
Garden.* Teens too old for a family book club? Grab your older
child's lit list from school and read the same books they're
reading. It'll give you more to talk about at stoplights.

Bozzo Family Fun File

For major fun, build an art room in your house. It
doesn't have to be fancy—in fact, it shouldn't be.
Find the creepiest, cruddiest corner of your basement

or garage or attic and make it somewhere safe for kids to create mess. Out of mess comes masterpiece, a creative spirit, and pride in making something come to life out of your mind's eye. We had art rooms when the girls were young where we stashed old record albums, wiggle eyes, paint, glitter, egg cartons—the stuff they needed to make their ideas take off. It's where we hosted birthday parties and playdates, where we made Christmas and birthday gifts, where the girls could go to be together or alone. Create a spray-paint station (with goggles). Let them pound nails. Let them stack and glue baby food jars and make papier-mâché. In my book, time spent not worrying about making a mess but rather turning imagination into real life is time well spent. Life is art!

▼▼▼▼▼▼▼▼▼▼▼▼▼▼▼▼▼▼▼▼▼▼▼▼▼▼▼▼▼▼▼▼▼▼

Fun from the Field

No room for an art room? Jessica B. says she will always remember making art in her grandma and pappap's basement with a black bag of art supplies her aunt brought along.

▲▲▲▲▲▲▲▲▲▲▲▲▲▲▲▲▲▲▲▲▲▲▲▲▲▲▲▲▲▲▲▲▲▲

Video Fun

Take advantage of technology. Videos are so fun and so easy to put together today with phones and iPads.

VIDEO INVITATIONS

What a fun way to set the stage for something you have planned. Find a song to sing to or send a funny video invitation.

Ages: Any   *Time:* Varies

MUSIC VIDEO

Next time you are looking for something to do, get the camera/phone rolling and put together a music video—lip-sync or belt it out for the world to hear. Musical instruments and cute costumes optional. Dancing required.

Ages: Any   *Time:* Varies

TIME WARP

You oughta be in pictures. Make your own black-and-white film and challenge your kids to channel their inner Charlie

Chaplin by making it a silent film. They'll love the high jinks and big, bold gestures.

Ages: 5–15   *Time:* Varies

VIDEO BIRTHDAY SHOUT-OUTS

Send faraway friends and family video birthday shout-outs you can e-mail, text, or post online.

Ages: 3–15   *Time:* Seconds

CHAPTER TWELVE

Big Fun on Big Holidays

New Year's Fun

There's no time like the big celebrations to create magic for little (and not-so-little) ones!

HOMEMADE THANK-YOU NOTES

We all get so much for the holidays. So how about making thank-you notes together? After all, gratitude is one of the best things you can teach your children. You can decorate thank-you notes with almost anything: buttons, felt, stamps, tinfoil, ribbons—even cereal. Let the kids get creative with ways to tell family how much they appreciate their presents and presence this year.

Ages: 3 and up   *Time:* 5–50 minutes

MAKE A FAMILY TIME CAPSULE

Chronicle the highlights of your year with a Family Time Capsule. Gather all the things that remind you of the past year.

Find a big tub—a jumbo plastic pretzel container from Costco works well. You can put in math tests, Halloween pictures, Valentine's Day cards, report cards, newspaper clippings—anything you want to archive—and then hide it somewhere to be discovered in ten or twenty years. Make note of where it's hidden if you want to be the family to discover it. Or happily forget about it so it can be discovered by another family down the line.

Ages: 5 and up   *Time:* 1–2 hours

NEW YEAR'S RESOLUTION BOARDS

It's easy to follow a goal when you can chart your yearly progress. List New Year goals on a decorated poster board, whether it's making the junior high orchestra, selling the most popcorn for the Boy Scout fund-raiser, or maybe getting straight As. Turn to it during the year as a reminder of what your aims are—even add to it as goals are realized and new goals pop up.

Ages: 6 and up   *Time:* 1 hour

NEW YEAR'S FAMILY FUN

Cut newspaper for homemade confetti and let the kids bang pots and pans on the porch to ring in the New Year. It sounds so simple, but it's still an exciting way to start the New Year with a bang.

Ages: 3 and up   *Time:* An evening to shred paper; seconds to toss it

SAY WHAT? HAPPY NEW YEAR!

Ring in the New Year in another language—Google makes it easy. Teach the kids how to say "Happy New Year" in a bunch of different languages. *Felice Anno Nuovo!*

Ages: 3 and up   *Time:* Minutes

RESOLUTION JARS

Make goal-setting fun with resolution jars. Grab an empty mayo jar or jelly jar. Write your goal on the jar with a paint pen or onto tape with a Sharpie marker. Every time you take steps toward your goal, put in a poker chip, a penny, or a few M&M'S.

Ages: 8 and up   *Time:* A few minutes

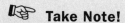 **Take Note!**

LOOK FOR A NEW (YEAR'S) TWIST!

Borrow a tradition from another country! We love this Croatian custom we do with friends on New Year's Day, where the oldest child gently spills a drop of wine on a candle to smother the flame. If the smoke goes straight up it signifies abundance. The tradition predicts the upcoming year in two ways—the abundance of food and the fortune of good health. The first attempt signifies abundance of food, the second health. Here are some other cultural traditions:

- In Spain, folks eat twelve grapes at the stroke of midnight for twelve happy months. Add a fun twist and take turns targeting the grapes into one anothers' mouths.

- In Greece, they bake a cake and hide a coin in it. Whoever finds the coin is the lucky one.

- In Colombia, folks walk around the block with an empty suitcase for a promise of new adventure in the new year.

- In China, they believe incorporating fish into the evening brings good fortune, so put a couple of colorful, fun fishbowls on the table that night.

  Ages: Any   **Time:** Varies

BALLOON DROP

Let the kids help you on this, or tackle it on your own. Blow up balloons and stick them inside a plastic tablecloth taped to the ceiling by the corners. At the stroke of midnight— or for little ones with an earlier bedtime, *kid*night—pull the tablecloth for a shower of balloons. For added fun, write out New Year's predictions on little slips of paper and put them inside the balloons before you blow them up. You can even add bits of confetti if you don't mind the cleanup. After the balloons drop, let the kids pop them for their predictions.

Ages: 2 and up   *Time:* 1 hour to set up; minutes to enjoy; 15 minutes for cleanup

POP, POP, POP INTO THE NEW YEAR!

Tape a sheet of bubble wrap onto the floor. You can find rolls at the office supply store or save from your packages throughout the year. At the stroke of midnight or *kid*night (you determine the time), stomp in the New Year—*pop, pop, pop!*

Ages: 2–4   *Time:* Minutes

NOON YEAR CELEBRATION

You can have all the New Year's hoopla for the little ones at noon—confetti, balloon stomp, Kool-Aid toast—and save the evening for the adult celebration.

Ages: 2–6   *Time:* 1 hour

Mardi Gras

Create your own Mardi Gras fun with . . .

HOMEMADE BEADS

Roll self-hardening clay into small balls; poke with a pencil. Let dry, paint, then string.

Ages: 3–8   *Time:* 30 minutes to make beads; overnight to dry; 30 minutes to string

MARDI GRAS MASKS

Make masks out of poster board. Decorate with glitter, feathers, anything fun you can find. Cut out two holes for eyes, add a ribbon to tie it on, and you are all set for your own Mardi Gras parade.

Ages: 3–12   *Time:* 45 minutes

CAPUCHONS

These large hats worn at the parades are fun and easy to make. Roll larger pieces of poster board into a dunce cap shape and staple to secure. Glue felt onto the hat and decorate with beads, rhinestones, or buttons.

Ages: 3–10   *Time:* 30 minutes

KING CAKE

Buy a king cake, or make your own. Kids love finding the baby stuffed inside. Even better, if you have a crowd, make king cupcakes and everyone gets a piece of good luck. Help little ones pinch their way through their cupcakes to make sure they don't choke.

Ages: 5 and up   *Time:* 1 hour to make; minutes to eat.

DOUBLOONS

The brightly colored coins thrown from Mardi Gras floats are called doubloons. Set up a coin toss for the kids with jars to flip them into. Or just fill a big jar with coins and have everyone guess the number inside.

Ages: Any   *Time:* A few minutes to 1 hour

GO NUTS WITH COCONUTS

Coconuts have been prevalent in Mardi Gras parades since 1910, when local painters started painting them and the folks on floats started handing them off to people in the crowds. Buy a couple of coconuts and paint them gold. You can also make them look like little faces.

Ages: 3–14   *Time:* 1 hour

LOOK FOR A TWIST ON MARDI GRAS FUN

In Italy they have a huge food fight on Mardi Gras; they call it the battle of the oranges. Depending on your appetite for mess, why not let the kids throw a few oranges!

Ages: 5 and up   *Time:* 30 minutes

PUPPETS

Puppets are such a big part of Mardi Gras parades, so why not pull them out for the little ones and have a puppet show? Or better yet, make your own sock puppets. Simply take a long sock, heel side up, and add yarn for hair and buttons for eyes. Slip your hand in to make the mouth and you are ready to go.

Ages: 3–8

Time: An afternoon

CRAYFISH RACES

Crayfish races are big in New Orleans, but there's no reason to limit the fun to NOLA. You can buy live crayfish online and make a simple race board—just a large piece of poster or stock board with a bull's-eye drawn on it. Put the crayfish in the center of the bull's-eye to start. If your crayfish crawls out of the bull's-eye first, you win. Keep playing for second, third, fourth. If you are racing lots of crayfish, put different-colored pieces of tape on their backs to keep track. If you're squeamish, you can wear rubber dishwashing gloves for handling.

Ages: Any　　*Time:* Seconds for the first round, but try as many rounds as you like!

Saint Patrick's Day

LEPRECHAUN FOOTPRINTS

Make green footprints by putting a couple of drops of washable paint on a paper plate. Stamp the side of your hand with the paint (make a fist first). Place the side of your hand (still fisted) down onto the floor.

Then dip a finger in the paint and make the toe prints at the top.

Ages: 1–5   *Time:* 5 minutes

GREEN MAGIC FUN

Buy some white carnations and put a few drops of green food coloring in the vase water, and the flowers will turn green overnight. You can either have the kids do this with you (a fun science project) or pretend it's leprechaun magic.

Ages: 2–8   *Time:* Overnight

PRANKSTER FUN

Some believe leprechauns come at night to pull pranks. Leave things overturned, hang pictures upside down, put dishes on the floor, or pull the toilet paper off its roll to make it look like you've been visited.

Ages: 2–8   *Time:* 15 minutes

EASY SHAMROCKS

Cut potatoes in half. Dip the white part into green paint, press out three shamrock leaves, and paint on a long stem.

Ages: 2–5   *Time:* 10 minutes

Fourth of July Fun

MAKE HOMEMADE FIREWORKS (SAFELY!)

Stretch balloons by blowing them up and then letting the air out. Use a funnel to stuff them with confetti. Then blow them up with a hand pump (or the old-fashioned way) and tie. When it comes time to celebrate America's birthday, give the kids pins or tacks and let them pop to their hearts' content.

Ages: 3–5   *Time:* 20 minutes to blow up a bunch; seconds to pop!

CONFETTI POPPERS

Take a six-ounce plastic water bottle and cut it about three inches from the lid. Cover the sharp edge of the top half with duct tape. Take off the lid and stretch a balloon over the opening so that it's on tight over the threads of the bottle neck. Cut confetti paper and pour it into your popper. Pull down the bottom of the balloon, holding the bottle neck with one hand, and let snap for a shower of confetti.

Ages: 3–6   *Time:* 30 minutes to make

THE STARS AT NIGHT (AND DAY) ARE BIG AND BRIGHT

Fill your front yard with stars. Make a star-shaped stencil out of cardboard. Lay the stencil on the lawn and spray the opening with water from a spray bottle. Dust flour over the opening—working with a sifter if you like—and you've got star power for the whole neighborhood to see.

Ages: 7 and up (or younger with lots of help)   *Time:* 1 hour

FIRECRACKER FLOWERS

Shred the ends of a coffee filter and secure with a rubber band a quarter of the way down, twisting the bottom into a stem. Kids can paint their flowers with watercolor paints.

Ages: 3–5   *Time:* 15 minutes

FLAG BOARDS

Make flag boards out of wood scraps, paint, white shoelaces, and nails! Or just make a flag out of an old white pillowcase.

Ages: 3–9   *Time:* 1 hour

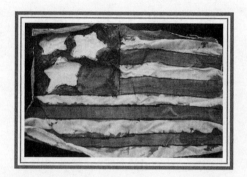

PIE-EATING CONTEST

Blueberry pie, anyone? Bake or buy pies and then line contestants up behind them. Contestants tie their hands behind their backs and eat to win. Yum.

Ages: Any   *Time:* Minutes

Halloween

Halloween is the day you can be anything! It's so fun to make a costume together, especially if your kids are young. There are a million ideas out there, and I encourage you to grab your sewing machines, glue guns, and wiggle eyes, and hit the thrift stores and the fabric stores—or, heck, the chicken wire store if you need to. Make a whole month of FUN.

THREE BLIND MICE COSTUME

This was such a great project, and to this day, it remains Ava's favorite Halloween costume. The girls worked an afternoon at a time. Younger kids worked alongside older sisters and friends because hot glue was involved and they were still too small to hot-glue by themselves. First we made the snoot (Ava laughed every time I said *snoot*, so of course I said it *a lot*). The girls took poster board and rolled it into a cone. We taped and stapled the poster board to make sure the snoot (see how I like to say it?) stayed in shape, then finished with a hot-glue gun (that's where the older girls came in). We hot-glued the cone along the edges of the opening of a black sweatshirt hoodie, then we traced and cut eye holes and a mouth. For ears we hot-glued paper plates to the hoodie. We glued sweat-shirt material onto the back of the ears and some of the front, leaving a blank space for a circle of pink felt. We glued black jersey material onto the snoot (there I go again!), gluing first, then recutting the eye and mouth holes on the snoot. We added white pipe cleaners for whiskers, a pink pom-pom for a nose, and of course sunglasses to the snoot. Black jersey pants topped it off, along with black fuzzy slippers with snipped pieces of pipe cleaner glued to them to make them look like furry paws. For canes, I bought brooms at the dollar store and twisted off the broom bristles, leaving just the white sticks. I went walking alongside the mice in our school parade dressed as the farmer's wife.

I got my inspiration for this from the YouTube video "How to Build a Mouse Costume" by Trevor Stone. I'd check it out if you are planning to make this costume.

Ages: 7 and up (with help)   **Time:** 3 or 4 playdates plus one shopping trip

HAUNTED GARAGE—BOO!

What to do for the teens in your family? Transform your garage into a haunted house—the kids will have a blast setting up and inviting friends over for a little spook. Good things to have on hand—a fog machine, skeletons, a bowl of grapes for feeling "eyeballs," spaghetti for "brains," clown masks, a coffin with a moving body in it, a recording of a chain saw, rubber or plastic body parts. The neighbors will be dying to get in for a fun night of fright.

Ages: 9 and up   *Time:* A couple of afternoons to set up; an evening (or two) to enjoy

UNCARVED PUMPKINS!

Who needs to carve when they can glue, glue, glue? Shells, pom-poms, Ping-Pong balls, candy corn—whatever you have on hand to make an uncut version of a jack-o'-lantern.

Ages: 2 and up   *Time:* 1 hour

Thanksgiving

PLAN A CHARLIE BROWN THANKSGIVING

If you can't do a traditional Thanksgiving dinner—or even if you can—throw a Charlie Brown Thanksgiving dinner with popcorn, jelly beans, pretzels, and buttered toast. Play the classic movie we all love, *A Charlie Brown Thanksgiving*, before or after the bird-brain feast—always a hit. Now, that's the Thanksgiving dinner the kids will remember.

Ages: 3–9   *Time:* 1 hour or so

LET'S TALK TURKEY

I made up this game to keep the conversation rolling at holiday dinners. Create a deck of conversation starters, like *What was your favorite vacation?* or *What's your best school memory?* Slip in a few cards with a turkey drawn on them. If someone draws a turkey card, they have to share an embarrassing or silly memory/story.

Ages: Any   *Time:* 1 hour or so

Fun from the Field

Want to find a Thanksgiving tradition that is easy peasy? Years ago when Becky S.'s kids were young, she bought a plain white tablecloth and invited all the folks around their table that year to sign the table-cloth, writing what they were most grateful for. For years, they traced their hands and made festive tur-keys next to their names and "what I am grateful for" items. Becky says she still brings it out every year for new signings. She created a rich tradition and some-thing she can easily bring on the road wherever their Thanksgiving travels take them.

GRATITUDE GOBLETS

Invite the kids to create Gratitude Goblets for everyone. Decorate goblets you find somewhere cheap, like a dollar store, with paint pens, writing out what everyone is most thankful for. Have kids make them for older relatives with sur-prise messages like, *Grandma, thanks for coming to my volleyball games. Mom, thanks for helping me ace that history test!* Alterna-tively, you can cut out poster board and make Gratitude Place Mats.

Ages: 8–15   *Time:* 20 minutes

SILLY GOOSE! NAME CARDS

Grab the Polaroid camera and strike your silliest poses for instant place cards. Clip them in clothespins for a simple holder.

Ages: 6–15   *Time:* 30 minutes

TURKEY CENTERPIECE

Make a fat ol' turkey centerpiece out of papier-mâché. Attach a big round balloon for the body to a long straight balloon for the neck and a small water balloon for the head. Cover with papier-mâché. After the papier-mâché dries, paint the turkey brown and add feathers to its backside, wiggle eyes, and a piece of red balloon for the wattle.

Ages: 3–8   *Time:* A couple of days

I AM GRATEFUL FOR

Take a plastic funnel and glue on Ping-Pong eyes, dotted with a Sharpie-marker-drawn circle, in the middle of the funnel. Glue colorful straws to the back end of the funnel. Write the things you are most grateful for on index cards, and glue the cards onto the straws. Top by gluing on a piece of candy corn for a beak.

Ages: 2–12   *Time:* 40 minutes

FAMILY PILGRIMAGE AND STORIES

Experts say that children who are most self-confident have what they call a strong intergenerational self. They know they belong to something bigger than themselves. The ones who know a lot about their families tend to overcome challenges better. Use Thanksgiving as a time to pull out the silly family stories to convey family history and develop a strong family narrative for your children, whether around a formal sit-down dinner or casually around the fireplace.

Ages: Any   *Time:* An evening

☞ Take Note!

What do you do if you are on the road for Thanksgiving? How do you make a hotel stay or a restaurant visit feel more like home? Here are my tips:

TINY TOUCHES

Sometimes a tiny touch means even more than the big traditional pomp and circumstance we put together at home. Wherever you roam, spice things up with scented candles (or even pumpkin bubble bath) to give everything a festive feel. Decorate hotel rooms or restaurant tables with a bit of nature. Send the kids out on a nature hunt for pinecones and sprigs of evergreen. Or warm a guest or hotel bed with an *I Am Grateful for You* pillowcase you can make or buy.

Bozzo Family Fun File

Reframe the Day: Create New Traditions

If you find yourself somewhere nontraditional over the holidays, take a step back and think about what is really important to you. Is it spending the day together creating memories, like a fantastic snow hike or long cross-country ski outing? Or a big meal? We spent a Thanksgiving in Beaver Creek, Colorado, one year and pushed hard to find the traditional turkey dinner at a restaurant. The dinner went nothing as we planned— it was actually a disaster, with bad food, bad service, and a crabby waiter—but the day leading up to it was magnificent: a surprise ten inches of snow on the

mountain and the first time my girls could actually spend the day skiing with us. We skied all day together as a family in the beautiful mountains. That was what I was most thankful for that day even when dinner went south. And it really changed the meaning of Thanksgiving for me. We were so rich that day— even before the dinner hour. Sometimes, it's not the meal or the traditions that count; it's the beauty of creating a new tradition and enjoying time together as a family in a different and exciting way.

Christmas

You could write a book on Christmas fun, so I'll just highlight a couple of my favorites.

MAKE ORNAMENTS OUT OF SALT CLAY

It is exciting to actually *make* a Christmas ornament, and it's simple to do. You can find a recipe for salt clay on the Internet. I used the most simple recipe (of course): two cups of flour, one cup of salt, one cup of cold water, and a half teaspoon of alum if you let your creations air-dry. Roll out the dough, use Christmas cookie cutters for shaping, poke a hook hole near the top with a pencil, air-dry or bake at 325 degrees Fahrenheit until they start to brown, let them cool, and paint them. You can make your ornaments super fancy with glitter and buttons. String with ribbon, and hang.

Ages: 2–8   *Time:* A snowy afternoon

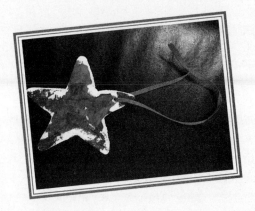

SALT CLAY SNOWMAN

Mine are missing wiggle eyes, one's arm is broken off—but still I put them in my china cabinet every year. Roll out three snowballs made of salt clay (recipe on previous page)—a head, middle, and bottom. Finish off with wiggle eyes, a speck of orange foam for the nose, stick arms, and a felt scarf.

Ages: 2–8   *Time:* A snowy afternoon

STRING POPCORN

This is an old-fashioned delight. All you need is a needle, thread, and a bowl full of popcorn. Thread needle and sew through the popcorn one kernel at a time until a string is formed.

Ages: 8–10   *Time:* A chilly evening

CHRISTMAS TREE PINECONES

Gather pinecones on the way home from school, or make a special trip to the woods with a basket. Paint them green, then add beads and pieces of sequins for ornaments.

Ages: 2–5   *Time:* A few minutes to gather; 20–30 minutes to paint

WINE BOX NATIVITY SCENE

Make a nativity scene out of a recycled wine box. Add a roof with the lid of the wine box, stain it or paint it brown, and add hay to the bottom. Make animals and people out of papier-mâché and wire hangers, with scraps of fabric for clothes and yarn for hair. For the Wise Men, use empty wine bottles, wooden balls for heads, lots of paint for facial features, and scraps of rich fabric for clothing.

Ages: 7–13   *Time:* Many winter afternoons

Fun from the Field

Do you feel yourself drowning come the holidays, never able to do all the things you want to do with the kids to make Christmastime memorable? There's nothing worse than the regret of not spending time together creating memories after the holiday fun has passed you by. Mary C. figured out a brilliant way to set her holiday-fun list in stone and create a wonderfully rich tradition her children look forward to every year. For the kids' advent calendars, instead of candy and gifts, Mary writes a holiday activity in each day's box. Whether it's ice-skating, tickets to *The Nutcracker*, making gingerbread houses, or wrapping presents, the kids discover what they will be doing *together* later that day when they open the day's door at breakfast.

CHAPTER THIRTEEN

Special Occasions

*Blow out a mundane holiday and create a new
reason to celebrate!*

Don't let all the big holidays hog the fun. Find ways to celebrate those smaller holidays too. Here are a few ideas for inspiration.

Elvis's Birthday: January 8

PLAY KINGS

All you need is a deck of cards!
Ages: 8 and up   *Time:* 1 hour

LOOK THE PART

Stick on sideburns and sunglasses at dinner. Serve hound
dogs (hot dogs!) and Elvis's favorite, peanut butter, banana,
and bacon sandwiches.
Ages: Any   *Time:* Dinner hour

JAILHOUSE ROCK

Crank up the Elvis tunes and have a sock hop! Do the Elvis Pelvis!

Ages: 3 and up   *Time:* 1 hour

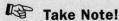 **Take Note!**

Ring in all the fantastic months of the year and celebrate their wonderfulness by reading the classic *Chicken Soup with Rice* by Maurice Sendak at the beginning of each month.

Martin Luther King Jr. Day: Third Monday in January

VOLUNTEER!

Martin Luther King Jr. Day has become a national day of service, so why not organize a fun volunteer effort for families? Make blankets for the homeless with your neighbors or organize a group to clean up litter on your local bike path. The National Day of Service website always has lots of good ideas on how to help out: www.serve.gov/?q=blog-terms/national-day-service.

Ages: Any   *Time:* 1 hour to a full afternoon

HIT YOUR LOCAL HISTORY MUSEUM

Ours hosts Martin Luther King Jr. and Rosa Parks impersonators, and presidents and first ladies on Presidents' Day. A terrific way to watch history come alive.

Ages: 3–13   *Time:* An afternoon or full morning

Groundhog Day Fun!: February 2

Personally, this is my favorite little holiday to make large. I don't know why—maybe because I'm oh so *over* winter by February 2, or maybe because little ones find fluffy groundhogs so cute. We read all the books we could find on Groundhog Day. After years of searching for a great Groundhog Day book, we found one we loved: *Groundhog Gets a Say* by Pamela Curtis Swallow. I think I've found a new favorite. Look for *Groundhog's Dilemma* by Kristen Remenar.

GROUNDHOG VERSION ONE

Fill a brown sock or the cut-off foot of a pair of panty hose with cotton or potpourri. Knot the bottom, leaving some slack for a tail. Paste on big wiggle eyes, Q-tips for large teeth, and a black or brown button for a nose.

Ages: 3–8   *Time:* 30 minutes

GROUNDHOG VERSION TWO

Brown felt works well for this little guy, but you can use any kind of fabric. Scrap corduroy painted brown provides a nice, stiff texture. Fold about a foot and a half of the fabric in half inside out and staple the sides, leaving the bottom unstapled. Turn right side out and stuff with cotton, then staple the bottom shut. Glue on Ping-Pong balls (don't you just love Ping-Pong balls?) as eyes—draw in the pupils with black Sharpie—cinch a bit of fabric on each top corner with a rubber band for ears, and add two painted Popsicle sticks for teeth and a big black button for a nose.

Ages: 3–8   *Time:* 30 minutes

GROUNDHOG DAY CAKE

What's a celebration without cake? Buy or bake a white cake and add your own adorable, edible groundhogs made out of mini candy bars. You can use Baby Ruth, Snickers, Milky Way—stick on brown M&M'S for ears and cheeks with brown frosting, add something pink for a nose (a pinch of Starburst works), and use white icing or fondant for eyes and teeth.

Ages: 3 and up   *Time:* 20 minutes; longer if you bake and frost your own cake

AND IF YOU GET GOOD NEWS?

Yes! Say good-bye to a long winter and hulloooo to a happy spring with *Welcome, Spring* signs, lots of smiley faces, and flowers the kids can make and put in the windows.

Ages: 3–8   *Time:* 30 minutes

Dr. Seuss's Birthday: March 2

*If you never did you should. These things are fun, and fun
is good.*

—Dr. Seuss

How I loved celebrating Dr. Seuss's birthday with the girls.
Such a fun excuse to pull out all his fantastic books. Here is a
fun way to pump up his birthday party.

CAT IN THE HAT

Paint a lightbulb to look like
the Cat in the Hat, adding wiggle
eyes and whiskers. Cut a toilet paper roll, leaving a quarter of the
tube as a stand. Top with an empty
yogurt container painted white
with thick red stripes; a circle of
cardboard makes a brim. (This
lightbulb is of course retired!)

Ages: 3–7
Time: 30 minutes

Cinco de Mayo: May 5

*Feel free to mix and match for both of these
Mexican holidays!*

TRADITIONAL MEXICAN KICKBALL

This is something many kids play in Mexican villages. Set up an obstacle course leading players under tables and chairs, in and out of cones, around trees, through tubes—even set up a backward zone. Select two teams, and the first person from each team kicks the ball through the obstacle course as fast as they can. When they finish, they pick up the ball and race it to the next player. The team that finishes first wins. Nerf balls are great for indoor play.

Ages: 5 and up   *Time:* 20 minutes

PIÑATA!

Who doesn't love a piñata? Fill with treats and hang from a tree. Kids each take a turn smacking it with a bat until it explodes!

Ages: 3–9   *Time:* About 15 minutes, depending on how many heavy hitters you have in the crowd

HOMEMADE MARACAS

Have the kids make their own maracas by putting dried beans into empty water bottles that they can decorate with stickers, ribbons, and markers.

Ages: 2–4   *Time:* 20 minutes

National Taco Day: October 4

MAKE TACOS FOR BREAKFAST!

Who says you have to wait for dinner? Use a waffle for the shell, stuff with scrambled eggs and bacon, and top with syrup!

Ages: Any   *Time:* 20 minutes

BATTLE OF THE TACOS!

Two players joust in a circle, each holding a wooden spoon with a hard taco shell balanced on the handle of the spoon. The object is to break your opponent's taco shell (while protecting your own). You can't touch the player—just their spoon and taco. The last taco shell still standing wins!

Ages: 8 and up   *Time:* A few minutes each round

SOME LIKE IT HOT

If you like it hot, you'll love this game! Line peppers up from mild to hot and have the kids challenge themselves to see how hot they can go! Have cold glasses of milk on hand to extinguish the fire!

Ages: 7 and up   *Time:* 15 minutes

Earth Day: April 22

CORN HUSK DOLL

Make an earth-friendly doll using your leftover corn husks. Soak the husks in water for about ten minutes. Wring dry, then shape a head on the top of the husk by tying with twine. Fashion an arm with a loose piece of husk, tying with twine, and thread through the husk body. Tie a waist, and make legs by tying ankles or leave bottom husks dangling to make a skirt. Glue on felt and fabric scraps for clothes and yarn for hair. Simple earthy fun.

Ages: 3–10   *Time:* About 1 hour

PAPIER-MÂCHÉ EARTH

You can make your own planet. Make paste by mixing one part flour with five parts water. Boil about three minutes and let cool so it won't burn you when you work with it. Dip strips of newspaper in the papier-mâché paste and place onto a round balloon. Let dry a day or so, then paint the oceans blue and continents green. Voilà, planet Earth.

Ages: 5–10 *Time:* 1 hour day one and 1 hour day two

BUILD A BIRD FEEDER

There are so many fun ways to make a bird feeder. For one, you can use a milk jug. Cut big holes in each side, leaving about two inches of plastic at the bottom of the jug. Fill the bottom of the bird feeder with birdseed. Birds will fly in and out of the feeder to grab seed. Decorate however you like. You can also make a bird feeder out of an empty two-liter bottle. Poke a couple of holes on the sides of the bottle and thread the handles of two or three wooden spoons through the holes you've made, leaving the spoon part flush against the bottle. Fill with birdseed, and the birdseed will come out onto the spoons for the birds.

Ages: 3–8 *Time:* 30 minutes

GROW A BEAN PLANT

Kids love to watch things grow. A bean plant is a good option because it grows quickly, so little ones don't have to wait long. Just put a damp paper towel in a jar and add a bean. It should sprout in a few days. Once you've grown your plant, add it to your outdoor garden.

Ages: 3–8 *Time:* A couple of days to 1 week

Johnny Appleseed Day: September 26

HOW 'BOUT THESE APPLES?

Apple. Apple. Apple. Go for apple everything on Johnny Appleseed Day. Juggle apples, bob for apples, go apple picking, and make applesauce, apple pie, apple pancakes, or apple muffins.

Ages: All   *Time:* Varies

HELLO, DOLLY!

Make apple dolls with dried apples—one of my favorite things to do as a Brownie when I was young. Peel an apple with a potato peeler, and core the apple. Draw facial features—eyes, nose, and mouth—on the apple with a pencil. Make sure the features are large, since the apple will shrink as it dries. Using your markings as a guide, carve the apple to look like a head and face. Combine equal parts lemon juice and salt in a bowl and soak the apple for about thirty seconds. Pat dry with a paper towel. Set the apple in a warm, dry place for a few days. Your apple should shrink, and the features you carved will distort. Add cloves for eyes. Attach the head to a wire hanger bent in half lengthwise, matching end to end. Make clothes and a kerchief with scrap fabric.

Ages: 3–10   *Time:* A couple of hours, with time in between for the apples to dry

PLANT A TREE

A fun way to honor Johnny Appleseed. Check with your local garden center to find the best type of tree to grow for your climate.

Ages: 3–10   *Time:* A few minutes

NEW YORK CITY

If you live close enough, spend the day in the Big Apple! If not, cue up a great New York City movie—like the 1973 classic *From the Mixed-Up Files of Mrs. Basil E. Frankweiler,* also a great read-along book. Also consider: *Night at the Museum, Home Alone 2: Lost in New York, Miracle on 34th Street,* or *Harriet the Spy.*

Ages: All   *Time:* An afternoon

▼▼▼▼▼▼▼▼▼▼▼▼▼▼▼▼▼▼▼▼▼▼▼▼▼▼▼▼▼▼▼▼▼▼▼▼▼

Fun from the Field

FRIDAY EVE!

What to do when you can't wait for Friday to fiiiiinallly come? Jennifer H. celebrates Friday Eve—also known as Thursday—with her family. Why not? Celebrate the countdown to F-R-I-D-A-Y! Ring it in like a New Year's Eve.

▲▲▲▲▲▲▲▲▲▲▲▲▲▲▲▲▲▲▲▲▲▲▲▲▲▲▲▲▲▲▲▲▲▲▲▲▲

Super Bowl Family Fun!

MAKE THE BIG DAY *OFFICIALLY* FUN!

On game day, have the little ones make their own press passes with index cards. Punch a hole through the top and string it around their necks. Let them draw or color them—or spell out PRESS with letter stickers. Play coach and let them interview you.

Ages: 3–9   *Time:* Minutes

TOUCHDOWN TRAY

The kids will have a field day with these. Line baking sheets with some green felt—or even better, a piece of Astroturf—paint field markers with a white paint pen, and erect goalposts using chopsticks or paint stirrers taped to the sides. Pile high with your favorite snacks and serve up food couch-side.

Ages: 3–7   *Time:* 20 minutes to make

FOOTBALL BINGO

Grab a few cookie sheets. Line with Astroturf (felt or foam paper works too). Then label each row and column with all the plays the kids should look for—a tackle, sack, punt, etc. Spectators turn into players as they race to complete a full row or column.

Ages: 4–8   *Time:* Game time

SWAG THE DOG

Make your own mascot—paint the dog with washable pet spray paint. Go for team colors or make up your own combination. Look for a paint that is veterinarian tested, dog safe, and easy to wash out.

Ages: 4–10   *Time:* 20 minutes

PREGAME TUG-OF-WAR

If you have some active, feisty kids in your Super Bowl group, throw a pregame or halftime game of tug-of-war. Just grab a Manila tug-of-war rope and get all the kids outside. Assemble teams, with each team grabbing on to the rope. Center the rope using a cone or other marker, then—*tug*.

Ages: 4 and up   *Time:* 20 minutes

YOU OUGHTA BE IN PICTURES!

Make your own football-themed photo booth. Set up a fun background—it could be poster board decorated with footballs or a square of artificial grass that you tape to the wall. Cut a square out of a piece of white poster board to look like the border of an instant photo, or a black piece of poster board to look like a frame. Set up a table with fun, simple props like eye black, football-shaped glasses, cardboard footballs attached to sticks, megaphones, "number one" foam fingers, helmets, plastic hot dogs, face paint, and jerseys—either real ones or ones cut out of cardboard. Strike a pose and let the "photographer" take your picture with an instant camera, or use an iPhone and print out with an iPhone printer.

Ages: All   *Time:* Throughout the day

TAILGATE IN THE LIVING ROOM

Grab an indoor grill or use the fireplace to cook up your favorite foods. Roast hot dogs, make s'mores, and grill chicken on an indoor grill. Even include a popcorn bar where kids can scoop their own bucket of fun victory victuals. Start with a huge tub of popcorn and a scoop, then line up all the toppings—Parmesan cheese, cinnamon, butter, salt, black pepper, and sprinkles in your favorite team's colors.

Ages: All   *Time:* Pregame

Fun Birthday Party Ideas

It's not hard to make a birthday seem big to a little one. For years and years I would look at this picture, thinking my family had a sign printed for my first big birthday party. I couldn't believe they would have had a sign made. Of course I now realize someone  cut streamer paper to spell out Happy Birthday. It really doesn't take much effort to make a big birthday impression on a small child!

It's so fun to blow out a birthday with a fun-to-plan party! Kids are little for only so long. Their interests change so quickly, so what kind of birthday should you plan? Here are a few I've had for my girls through the years. Borrow bits and pieces, or take the whole cake.

▼▼▼▼▼▼▼▼▼▼▼▼▼▼▼▼▼▼▼▼▼▼▼▼▼▼▼▼▼▼▼▼▼▼▼▼

Fun from the Field

Yes, birthday parties *can* be expensive—but they don't have to be. If you want to host an American Girl doll party but don't want to spend a fortune at the American Girl store, take a page from Jorie C.'s book. For her seventh birthday party she hosted a ladies' lunch for a group of gals and their dolls at her house. She put out all her American Girl toys as well as a beauty chair borrowed from friends so there would be a lot to play with. The little ladies sat at one table and the dolls sat at a miniature table with miniature food put out for them. The guests took turns doing their dolls' hair with supplies Mom bought. And each girl went home with a pair of Target doll shoes. A fantastic time for a fraction of the price of a traditional American Girl party hosted at the store.

▲▲▲▲▲▲▲▲▲▲▲▲▲▲▲▲▲▲▲▲▲▲▲▲▲▲▲▲▲▲▲▲▲▲▲▲

PRINCESSES AND PIRATES

If your little ones love to dress the part for parties, host a Princesses and Pirates party. Guests can fluff out those princess dresses or walk the plank in pirate hats, bandanas, and eye patches while waving their swords.

Ages: 3–5   *Time:* Party time!

MADELINE

Throw a Madeline party with simple yellow hats and blue smocks. You can make your own smocks with rectangular pieces of bright blue felt tied with a red ribbon. Paint little wooden houses sawed out of scrap wood. Make a hat cake with two rounds, one larger and thinner and a thicker, smaller one on top. Ice with bright yellow frosting and tie on a large black ribbon. Decorate with suitcases, Eiffel Towers, and blue-and-white striped tablecloths.

Ages: 3–5   *Time:* Party time!

BIRTHDAY HALFTIME

Count six months or 182 days from your family members' birthdays and mark the calendar to keep the good times rolling with a half-birthday celebration.

Ages: Any   *Time:* Party time!

Party like a rock star.

ROCK AND ROLL

Turn your garage, basement, or local park pagoda into a raging rock-and-roll party. Bring out fun outfits, tattoos, and music, music, music. Older kids love playing DJ.

Ages: 6 and up   *Time:* A few hours

SCIENCE PARTY

Clear out the basement and set up stations with easy-to-do science experiments. The kids don plastic lab aprons and goggles and take turns measuring, experimenting with magnets, and looking at the sky with a telescope. Other possible activities? Making rockets, going on a bug hunt, trying out science experiments, and eating homemade Hot Lava Volcano Cake.

Ages: 4 and up   *Time:* A couple of days to set up; 2–3 hours for the party

HOT LAVA VOLCANO CAKE

Bake three cakes in large, medium, and small clay mixing bowls.

Let the cakes cool, then stack them on top of each other, largest on the bottom, smallest on top. They don't have to be perfect—in fact it's better if they look a little jumbled and rocky. So let them lump into each other, gently shaping as you go.

Frost with mud-colored frosting (chocolate is our favorite).

Melt a couple of packages of red Jolly Ranchers in a saucepan. Pour out on a foil-lined baking sheet in shapes that look like spurting hot lava. Let cool, loosen, then stick into the cake near the top of the volcano—like lava erupting. Right before the party, grab some dry ice (try the fish store) and put it around the cake, using rubber gloves because the ice will burn you if you touch it with bare hands. If you go for the dry ice, make sure the cake is put up high and an informed adult serves it. Do not touch the dry ice.

HARRY POTTER

Throw a Harry Potter birthday party—with capes (easy to make with a rectangle of felt and Velcro tab), Harry Potter glasses, red ties, a trip to the enchanted forest (or local woods) to search for dragon eggs, and a broomball game on the driveway or in the basement. Send party invitations by stuffed (animal) owl. You can usually find inexpensive ones at the dollar store. Attach an official Hogwarts invitation to the owl—a piece of paper previously dipped into cooled tea and dried, then wrinkled and burned a bit at the edges. You can find the Hogwarts logo on the Internet. Request an RSVP by owl. The guests will love flying their owls back with a response. With adults or big siblings' help, sort the guests into houses using the Sorting Hat. Set up an old-fashioned feast in the dining room complete with candelabras, silver-plate chargers, Hogwarts crests, goblets of butterbeer, chocolate frogs, and lots of rubber snakes and mice. Make wands out of the cardboard taken off dry-cleaning hangers. Make bubbly potions with vinegar, baking soda, and food coloring. Watch the movie and cap off the enchanted evening by letting the guests sleep over in front of a roaring fire(place).

☞ Take Note!

Not crazy about hosting a birthday party at home? There are so many cool places to have a party, and I don't just mean the roller rink and the bowling alley. You just have to think outside of the birthday box. Tamara B. hosted her son's Batman party in a cave. Holy Batcave! Can you imagine being in a real cave for a birthday party?

A SERIES OF UNFORTUNATE EVENTS

Throw a Series of Unfortunate Events party in honor of the beloved series. Serve lots of lemony treats (Lemonheads, lemonade) for Lemony Snicket. Have guests sit in a circle and spin a bottle; when the bottle points to you, you pick a fun disguise—a chicken beak, a pig nose, a feathered cap, funny teeth. Go round after round, players layering their disguised look. Play the evil laughing game: A blindfolded player stands in the middle of a circle, spins round and round, and when she stops she points at a player in the circle. That player gives her best evil laugh, and the blindfolded player must guess who it is.

Ages: 9–11   *Time:* Party time!

SLUMBER PARTY CAKE

It's easy to make this adorable slumber party cake. Slice Twinkies in half for sleeping bags, and use vanilla wafers for the sleepers' faces. Decorate faces with icing gel for features and hair, and frost the Twinkies. Arrange the "sleeping kids" on any cake frosting over the sleeping bags in different colors and add sprinkles or colored cake sugar.

Ages: All   *Time:* About 1 hour

Have your kids hand-deliver their party invitations when they are little, if you can. It gives them an opportunity to learn how to invite someone over.

CRIME-SCENE PARTY

Turn your house into a crime scene and CSI investigation. Make a cryptic invitation using letter stickers, fake blood, a bit of crime-scene tape, and fingerprints. Photocopy the invitation and deliver copies anonymously, directing guests to a website. Websites are easy to make using programs like Weebly. Set up a simple one that gives the guests the who, what, and where on the party and briefs them on the crime they are being invited to help solve. What can your crime be? Try "Who stole Mom's cookie recipe?" Have the kids help you set up a crime scene in your kitchen—flour everywhere, fake fingerprints, fake blood. Dump out a recipe box and scatter recipe cards with one missing—the family cookie recipe. Tape off the area with crime-scene tape. Hide other clues that hint at who could have stolen the recipe, and wait for the party to begin. As guests arrive, hand out little detective kits—a notebook, a magnifying glass. Brief guests when they arrive in a room where you have clues on exhibit and a rundown of your suspects. Pool your neighbors or family members to play suspects by reading a brief you

hand them before the party. They'll have fun acting out their parts in a funny whodunit. Give the kids time to scour the crime scene for clues and question the suspects, and then gather the group to hash out the evidence and come up with their own theories of who stole the cookie recipe.

Ages: 11–15   *Time:* A day to prepare; a party to enjoy

DOUBLES

Plan a doubles celebration in some form when your not-so-little one turns ten. It doesn't have to be a full-blown party but just a small way to sneak in some doubles fun throughout the day, say, at the breakfast table or even at dinner that night. Throw Dubble Bubble and Doublemint gum on the table. And of course lots of pairs of dice to play doubles. For eating, serve two of everything—two mini hot dogs, two slices of apple, two carrots.

Ages: 10   *Time:* Varies

Taking your party on the road? Sometimes keeping track of twenty kids in public can be a challenge. Try making T-shirts for all the guests for easy recognition.

Fun and Games for Family Picnics and Barbecues

LAWN TWISTER

Turn your front yard into a Twister board. Find a nice patch of lawn to plot out your Twister board. Cut a circle out of a pizza box and use it as a guide to spray-paint rows of dots on the lawn in Twister colors—green, yellow, red, and blue. Keep the spray paint on the grass away from plants. While the dots are drying make a paper-plate spinner. On each quarter section of a paper plate, paint dots of the corresponding colors from the lawn, then fasten an arrow to your paper plate with a paper fastener to serve as a spinner.

Ages: 5 and up   *Time:* 30 minutes to paint the yard; 30 minutes to play!

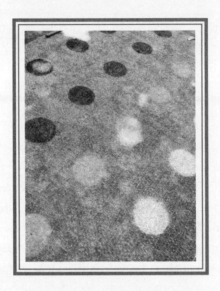

KOO KOO KA CHOO: THE EGG MAN RACE

On your marks, get set—put those hard-boiled eggs (or even golf balls) on spoons. Line racers up at the starting line and it's a race to the finish. Runners must run to the end line keeping the eggs on their spoons and one hand behind their backs. If you drop your egg, you must start again. First egg man who crosses the finish line—hand still behind back—wins!

Ages: 3–8   *Time:* 30 minutes

CHAPTER FOURTEEN

Bonding

The only gift is a portion of thyself.
—RALPH WALDO EMERSON

Carving Out Fun with One Child

Make a date with your child for some quality one-on-one time. Experts say that one-on-one time is a good idea for kids.

I am big on one-on-one time because you can tailor the fun to the little's one's Fun Print. Before I was a mom, I was an aunt, and I'd schedule little afternoon dates or overnights with my nieces and nephews. We went on riverboat rides, went horseback riding, tried skiing, visited the weather station at the TV station where I worked, went to museums, and had picnics. When my girls were all in preschool I put them in school on different days. (As a freelance writer, I was able to do my work at night.) It made things a bit nuttier for me but gave me the chance to have priceless one-on-one time with each child.

LITTLE SPORT'S DAY

Pack up your ball and bat, Frisbee, even skateboards or Rollerblades for an all-around sports day. Score a home run by catching a nighttime or afternoon baseball game.

Ages: 3–10   *Time:* A fun afternoon

NATURE LOVER

Spend the day in the great outdoors with your little adventurer, hiking, biking, fishing—even having a picnic outdoors. Send them on a scavenger hunt for pinecones, fossils, and certain types of leaves. If you start on the late side, pack a blanket and top the day by stargazing.

Ages: 3–10   *Time:* A fun afternoon—and maybe part of the evening

LITTLE LEARNER

Start the day at the library—catch a program together or just stockpile the books. Then spend the day hitting the local museums!

Ages: 3–8   *Time:* A fun afternoon

BUDDING ARTIST

Take art on the road. Set up an easel, grab paints and paintbrushes, and paint beautiful vistas in your backyard or beyond. Could be the sun over the lake, a grove of trees, or even a field of wildflowers. Cap the day off with a visit to your local art museum.

Ages: 3–9   *Time:* A fun afternoon

GREEN THUMB

Spend the morning together picking strawberries at one of the local farms, then hit the garden store for seeds and dirt and start your own vegetable garden together. Or grow houseplants from seedlings. Then head over to your local conservatory or an urban garden.

Ages: 3–8   *Time:* A fun afternoon

▼▼

Fun from the Field

Stay in your pj's all day? Victoria S. used to do this with her girls when they were little. They'd declare it pajama day and Victoria said she'd turn off the phones and they would just spend the day together, starting with pancakes cut into animal shapes for breakfast.

▲▲

Making Intergenerational Time More Fun and Rewarding

A happy family is but an earlier heaven.

—GEORGE BERNARD SHAW

FAMILY GAME: MAKE YOUR OWN GAME USING FAMILY HISTORY

*I made this game up. It's easy to make and
really helps kids to cherish family.*

Start with a huge piece of poster board or mount board. Cut family pictures (or photocopies of those pictures) to make spaces on the board. Pick tokens that represent the characters in your household—maybe a Matchbox car for the teen always wanting to borrow the keys or a miniature ballet shoe for the dancer in the house. Draw a path made out of spaces with some of the spaces marked "?" If when you roll the dice, you land on a "?," you have to answer a question for a chance to roll again

and continue down the path. Fuzzy dice make it more fun. The question cards are fun to make up. Use index cards to write the questions on. You can ask all kinds of things, like "Name the player to your right's favorite sport." Or, "Where were Grandma and Grandpa married?" Or "Who did Uncle Larry take to the prom?" Any question about your family members or family history is fair game. You can keep making a new batch of family questions so you can refresh the game over the years.

Ages: 5 and up   *Time:* About a day to make; 30 minutes to play

FAMILY PHOTO ALBUM

At your next family get-together, make a family photo album. Either have everyone bring photos and paste them in scrapbooks, or take pictures of the photos on phones or a central iPad, then upload them to a digital photo book site like Shutterfly to quickly create a book honoring your family history.

Ages: 8 and up   *Time:* A couple of hours or full afternoon

WRITE YOUR GRANDPARENTS' LIFE STORY

One of my cousin's and my favorite things to do together when we were growing up was interviewing each other on a tape recorder. Oh, to have that cassette tape today! Have the kids set up interviews with their grandparents next time you are all together. Record them and challenge the kids to write their grandparents' life story, to be shared at the next get-together.

Ages: 5 and up   *Time:* 1 hour

THIS IS YOUR LIFE WITH GRANDMA AND POP

Gather fun costumes and props. Set up a stage with a curtain. Affix some string from one wall to another in a small room or small corner and drape a light cloth or sheet over it, stapling or pinning the lip. Have Nanny and Pap sit on the couch. Each child takes a turn standing behind the curtain and shouts out clues as to which character they are in their grandparents' life. They reveal themselves in their costume when there's a correct guess. If my kids were playing this with their grandparents, they might dress like a milkman (or simply hold a quart of milk) and say something like "I was your kids' hero for many years, giving them pieces of ice from my milk truck, and you asked me to fetch your husband from down the street when it was time for you to go to the hospital to have your seventh child." Answer: Carl the Milkman.

Ages: 5 and up   *Time:* 1 hour

POLKA!

Put on some of the older generation's favorite music, move the coffee table, and ask grandparents, great-aunts, and great-uncles to lead the kids in some of the dances they enjoyed back in the day.

Ages: Any   *Time:* Varies

SPIN THE VINYL

Do your kids even know what a record album is? Spin the vinyl while you're rolling up the carpet! Grab a turntable and have the relatives bring over their favorite albums from back in the day or raid the local Goodwill and build your own arsenal of retro fun. TV show theme songs are always a hoot. And don't forget to look inside the album jacket, where they usually print the lyrics, so you can sing along.

Ages: Any   *Time:* A fun evening

MAKE FAMILY RECIPES TOGETHER

Invite Grams to put together her own cooking show in the kitchen with the kids as her students. If you want to revisit the recipe later, record it on video and share it with relatives on YouTube or Vimeo. For extra fun buy some splashy aprons and chef hats.

Ages: Any   *Time:* Varies

Fun from the Field

Brian C.'s mother passed away before anyone learned her sauce recipe. Sometimes a family dish provides lots of comfort and keeps family traditions alive long after loved ones have left us. Why not create a family cookbook with recipes, family stories—even old pictures? It's a great project for slightly older kids to tackle with grandparents, aunts and uncles, and cousins.

Fun from the Field

What if you seldom see all those faraway relatives? Teresa H. has a wonderful idea for keeping loved ones top of mind for little ones. Her family names the parks they visit after seldom-seen family members: "Want to go to Grandma's Park or Uncle Herbert's Park after school?" A simple but fun way to honor those you hold dear but who aren't so near.

Create Family Memories with Traditions

Traditions are the glue that holds
families together.

Bozzo Family Fun File

The Night Before Christmas

While my husband was growing up, his father read *The Night Before Christmas* to his seven kids every year. We have the book today. My husband considers it his greatest family heirloom. So of course, we've done the same—Matt reads *The Night Before Christmas* to our girls every year. And I display the photos of him reading to them at Christmastime. When all the girls leave home, I will have a coffee table book made out of the pictures.

HIDE THE PICKLE

Here is a dilly of a German tradition: Buy a pickle ornament for the tree and put it on the tree on Christmas Eve after the little ones go to bed. First one to spot the pickle on Christmas morning gets a year of good fortune.

Ages: All   *Time:* A few minutes

AROUND THE HORN

Try this fun family tradition. The birthday person of honor in our house gets the spotlight at dinner. Go around the horn, taking turns telling the birthday boy or girl why they are loved and what makes them great.

Ages: All   *Time:* 10 minutes

A WONDERFUL BIRTHDAY WAKE-UP

When the birthday boy or girl falls asleep at night, everyone sneaks into their room to decorate. Use balloons, streamers, and flowers; stack presents; hang signs. It's always good if you can do a lot of sign making and balloon blowing up beforehand. It's hard, but shh—be as quiet as mice. No giggling. In the morning, *surprise!* They wake up to birthday hoopla!

Ages: All   *Time:* Yawn, 20 middle-of-the-night minutes

Bozzo Family Fun File

Juicy Gum Tree

My aunt Dee would grow a Juicy Fruit tree for her kids' birthday parties. She'd have her little ones plant a pack of gum a couple of weeks before the big day. That morning, there would be a rubber tree plant on the table with packs of Juicy Fruit gum for all us kids to pick. It was so magical and fun. I remember dreams of my own Juicy Fruit tree growing spontaneously in my backyard. Of course as we grew older and noticed the Scotch tape on the leaves, we still loved the memory and keeping the secret safe for the little ones. You don't have to wait for birthdays—fun like this is meant for ordinary days, too.

Ages: 2–8   *Time:* 20 minutes

Join-the-Club Fun

Everyone likes to feel like they belong to something, so why not turn family fun into an exclusive club? Not only is it great to form a group, but a club also means making time together a regular thing. Not sure where to start? Here are some ideas.

A NEIGHBORHOOD CARD CLUB

Roving card table and snacks. Make it Bridge, Euchre, Hearts, Uno. If you set one table for kids and one for grownups it makes it a family affair.

A COLLECTING CLUB

Like to collect? A few can play at that game! Start collecting as a family or with a group of friends.

A MOVIE CLUB

House to house or theater to theater—these are great fun, especially in the winter months. My favorite time? Just before they roll out the red carpet for the Academy Awards so you know who you are rooting for!

CHAPTER FIFTEEN

On the Road

Things to Do Between There, Here, and Everywhere

COOPED-UP CAR FUN

Dreading the thought of taking a looonnnng car ride with the kids? Break up the ride with this clever idea. Wrap little presents for the kids before they leave—small toys and activities to keep them occupied. Ideas include little toy games like mini Rubik's Cubes, crossword puzzle books, a new toy car, or a Barbie with outfits. Each hour on the hour, the kids get to unwrap a present. Voilà! A new activity captures their interest and prevents boredom. Good for plane rides too!

Ages: Any   *Time:* A car ride

GO DOWN TO CHINATOWN

Hit Chinatown for a feast of culture and new foods. Kids love trying new things—bubble tea is usually a hit. Try your hand at reading Chinese. And, while you are there, let them find out the year they were born—the Year of the Snake? The Year of the Ox? The Year of the Monkey?

Ages: Any   *Time:* An afternoon or evening

TRAVEL TREASURE MAPS

These are a huge hit and oh-so-easy to make. You'll love the on-the-road learning with travel treasure maps you make for the kids before you leave on a big (or small) trip. Grab a clipboard and paper and write out clues for your little travelers. Write out questions like "What is the capital of the state we are visiting?" and tasks like "Get the pilot's autograph." You can use pictures pulled off the Internet for prereaders, like a yellow cab or "I heart NY" shirt. Kids love toting their clipboards (makes them feel important), marking off items as they discover them along the way.

Ages: 3–12   *Time:* All the downtime on vacation

BACKSEAT BINGO

If a holiday weekend means lots of time in the car, you can still take fun on the road with you. Backseat Bingo is easy to make and fun to play. Collect as many cookie sheets as you have kids playing. I like the smaller ones you find at the dollar store. Cover a cookie sheet with colored paper, a thin piece of felt, or foam paper. Make squares with markers, and draw, write, or put stickers in each square of the things you may see along the way—a yellow car, a stop sign, a bridge, a railroad crossing, a red truck. As kids spot the items on their bingo card, they mark that square with a magnet. First to get a row across, down, or diagonal shouts out *bingo!*

Ages: 4 and up   *Time:* A long or short car ride

STORY BAGS

Have a long car ride ahead? Story bags keep the conversation rolling. Fill paper bags with ordinary items from home and one by one passengers continue a narrative with an item they pull out of a bag. For example, if you pull out an envelope, start your tale with something like, "The money mysteriously disappeared from the envelope marked *urgent....*" Then let the next passenger continue the story with the random item they pick. You can play again and again—because the story is always changing.

Ages: 5 and up   *Time:* A long or short car ride

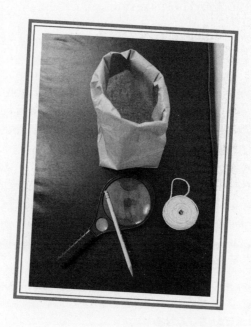

MOVING MOVIE!

Instead of packing a movie for the car, have the kids make their own movie—either at home before you hit the road or, even better, during your travels. You can find video cameras for kids as young as three, or if you have a carload of teens, have them shoot on their phones. Pack a pocket-sized projector so the kids can play their finished movie against the back of the front seat (tape on a piece of white paper) on the way home. Great to keep for a trip down memory lane years later.

Ages: As young as 3 (with help); great for teens

Time: A long or short car ride

▼▼▼▼▼▼▼▼▼▼▼▼▼▼▼▼▼▼▼▼▼▼▼▼▼▼▼▼▼▼▼▼▼▼▼▼

Fun from the Field

On their last four vacations in northern Michigan, Abel S.'s kids conceptualized, shot, and edited a music video as a memento of their week. Some of the footage is staged, as it involves lip-synching the lyrics to portions of a song (selected by his daughters). All the footage was shot on iPhones, and the girls used iMovie to edit the video. Then Abel helped them add graphics. He says watching the videos always brings back memories of their wonderful vacations and all the FUN they had together.

▲▲▲▲▲▲▲▲▲▲▲▲▲▲▲▲▲▲▲▲▲▲▲▲▲▲▲▲▲▲▲▲▲▲▲▲

ROOFTOP TRAVEL DIARY

Attach a map or draw one on felt and secure it to the roof of your vehicle. Let little ones trace the ride with a toy car

(Velcro attached underneath) or a cardboard cutout of a car they can tape to the map as you make your way down your many roads.

Ages: 2–4   *Time:* A long car ride

BUNDLED BOOK FUN

Bundle learning and fun for kids by making your own story kits with popular books. Find little toys that help them act out the story they are reading or you are reading to them and tuck them inside a bag with the book. If you don't have a ton of time, you can find kits like this online. A large Ziploc bag works well—or even a brown bag. Just put in the book, say, *Frog and Toad*, and little toys like toy frogs, finger puppets, or a miniature toy bike—anything that will help them act out the story. It's a great way for the kids to *play* with reading.

Ages: Prereader–7   *Time:* 1 hour

FOR NAMESAKE!

Have a long car ride with the kids? Download songs with their names in them—little kids love this. They'll beg you to play *their* song again and again.

Ages: 3–8   *Time:* A very giggly 2½ minutes

HIKING HERE, THERE, AND EVERYWHERE!

Want a way to stretch your legs and create fun family memories? Plan a midtrip hike on that next road trip. Or, if your kids are little, use your GPS to search out the nearest park or playground when you stop to fill up your gas tank.

Ages: 5 and up   *Time:* 1–2 hours

> ### Bozzo Family Fun File
>
> On our way to Pittsburgh to see family, we've gone a different way each time so that we could stop for a hike in beautiful West Virginia. The landscape is mesmerizing in the fall. Just make sure you check your dates for deer-hunting season.

SCIENCE STOP-BYS (OR DRIVE-BYS)

If you belong to your local science museum, your membership might be reciprocal at science museums across the country through the ASTC Travel Passport Program, meaning you can visit many other science museums at least ninety minutes away from your home museum for free! Check out www.astc.org/passport/ and see if there is a science museum en route for your next road trip or destination.

Ages: 3 and up   *Time:* 1–2 hours

MAKE A QUICK BRAIN-POP STOP

Scour the map or do a quick Google search to find out neat stops to discover along the way. Study a historic landmark like Lincoln's boyhood home. Marvel at a roadside wonder like the Centralia, Pennsylvania, mine fire, where a coal seam fire has been burning three hundred feet underground since 1962. Or try a neat factory tour like the Jelly Belly factory tour in Fairfield, California. Once we were able to stop and hike to a coal shaft. We could actually look inside, and it was so much cooler and wetter and darker in the coal shaft—a good way to explain the working conditions from back in the day.

Ages: 3 and up   *Time:* 1–2 hours

CHILDREN'S MUSEUMS

Children's museums are a wonderful resource for children and busy parents who don't always have a lot of time to set up learning and fun. The Children's Museum of Indianapolis is the world's largest children's museum, and if you are driving through Indiana, it's a terrific stop that boasts five floors of learning for all ages. A yearly pass makes short visits worth the money. And ask about family memberships.

Ages: 1–10   *Time:* 1–2 hours

ROADSIDE RADIO SHOW

Bring along a tape recorder (remember those?) or an iPad or phone that records audio and challenge your kids to come up with a roadside radio show, pointing out all the cool things you spot along the way—the World's Biggest Ball of Twine?

Ages: 11–15   *Time:* A long drive

ROADSIDE PICNICS

I love a roadside picnic on a nice day! It's a great way to stop and enjoy time together outside. All you need is a tablecloth.

Ages: All   *Time:* A leisurely lunch hour

A STOCKED CAR

Stock your car with items to make the trip more fun. Glow and go: glow-in-the-dark necklaces and bracelets make a night trip more exciting for little ones and provide the perfect personal night-light. Window markers are fun for back-window doodling, and they are easy to wipe clean with a baby wipe.

Big, Spectacular, Fantastic Fun

Pull out all the stops! Sometimes you just have to say *what the fun*—and pull out the big-guns fun. A big burst of fun is the conductor for a happy life. It creates forever family and personal memories that keep you smiling for years to come. Here are some of the splashier things we've done as a family to give you a bit of inspiration.

FEEDING TIGERS

At Out of Africa Wildlife Park, outside of Phoenix, they let you feed tigers. Oh, yes they do! Just before you zip-line past giraffes. It's also where you can kiss a giraffe!

ROAD LOOPS

Take a road trip together—and plan to come home a different way. I call it a Road Loop. Road Loops loop your travel, double your F-U-N, and make the trip go so much faster because the scenery is changing.

FAMILY CAMP

Try out a weekend or weeklong family camp. The YMCA is a good place to start.

DUDE!

Check into a dude ranch. Our favorite family dude ranch is Horseshoe Canyon Ranch in Jasper, Arkansas.

ROCK CONCERT ON A SCHOOL NIGHT

Take the kids to a rock concert on a school night.

HIKE THE GRAND CANYON

Try hiking to Cedar Ridge on the South Kaibab Trail, which drops about a thousand feet into the Grand Canyon. Crazy-big fun—and hold on to your socks, because there's not much else to hold on to; it is a steep, steep, scary descent. And the hike back makes *that* look easy!

GO HANG GLIDING!

Really fun to do at Kitty Hawk, where the Wright brothers mastered flight!

TAKE A TRAPEZE CLASS

Crazy-fun! And really gets you out of your comfort zone!

TRY GLAMPING

Who says you have to rough it to spend time with your kids in the great outdoors! With beds, chandeliers, and breakfast delivery, it's not your grandmother's camping, for sure. You get the quality time together without all the hassle of setup.

HIKE SLEEPING BEAR DUNES

With sand dunes so high, you can see them from outer space, Sleeping Bear Dunes in Empire, Michigan, is the ultimate dune climb.

! *FUN FACT:*

Plan a vacation and quadruple your happiness. Researchers from the Netherlands studied the effect vacations have on overall happiness and how long that happiness lasts. They found that the largest boost comes from simply planning it. Vacation anticipation boosted happiness for a whopping eight weeks.

Bozzo Family Fun File

The Road Less Traveled Is Often Traveled by Horse and Buggy

"Now, who the heck would want to stay overnight at a place with no electricity in July?" That's what my husband asked me a couple of summers ago when Shannon, my best friend from college, and I planned to stay with an Amish family with our kids on the way home from our Washington, DC, road trip. Shannon is my Thelma. She is an amazing teacher (and amazing mom), and she is always willing to go along with my wacky road-trip plans if it means teaching the kids something new. So that summer on our way home from Washington, DC, we took a turn off the beaten path to a place where life is purposely simple and the road less traveled is mostly traveled by horse and buggy—Fredericksburg, Ohio, which lies in the heart of the world's largest Amish population. The kids couldn't wait. It was going to be the highlight of our seven-day road trip.

For most of our ride into Ohio, we talked about what it meant to be Amish. I answered their questions with what I could find on Wikipedia. But as in life, true answers came through experiencing things firsthand. That night, we quickly settled in by the glow of gaslights. The next day we tried cow milking, helped tend to farm chores, went on a buggy ride, and made our way into town to go to an animal swap meet, where you literally can buy a pig for a couple of ducks. We rounded out the day with a tour of an Amish one-room schoolhouse and one last buggy ride. It was such a fun side trip for us on our way back to our bustling life of modern convenience.

SUBWAY RIDES

Take the New York subway everywhere—especially fun for little riders.

Ages: Any   *Time:* Varies

Bozzo Family Fun File

Welcome Spontaneity—Always, Always, Always

One warm summer night, on the way home from dinner with the kids for our wedding anniversary (the girls used to always ask, "Where are we going on our anniversary?"—so funny), we spotted a sidewalk music fest where instructors were teaching folks how to tango. We parked and walked over, and the five of us danced our anniversary night away!

CHAPTER SIXTEEN

Fun in Any Weather

Try a Little Beach-Bum Fun

Play is the work of the child. —MARIA MONTESSORI

SAND ART

Create masterpieces in the sand: bring paper and glue to the beach and let the kids make sand art! Just "draw" with the glue on your paper, sprinkle on dry sand, and pour off the excess. Try mixing the sand with food coloring too for fun hues.

Ages: 2–8   *Time:* Minutes

MESSAGE IN A BOTTLE

Put a message in a bottle and send it out to sea. Messages can be cryptic, like "To whoever finds this—have a nice day," or they can be specific, like "If you find this message, mail it to the Bozzo family with the date and location. We'd love to hear from you."

Bring along a little glass or plastic bottle with a cork or lid, a sheet of notepaper, and a Ziploc bag. Put your note in the Ziploc bag inside the bottle before closing it and tossing it into the water.

Ages: 4–10   *Time:* 20 minutes

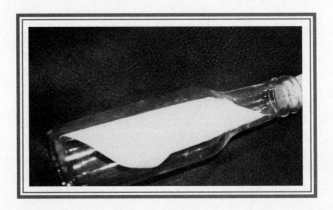

☞ Take Note!

Take along a great beach read. Try *Pirate Patch and the Treasure Map* by Helen Parker and *Message in a Bottle* by Susan K. Horn for kids about five and *Three Times Lucky* by Sheila Turnage for kids ten and older.

TREASURE HUNT

Ever wish you could discover hidden treasure?

Fill a treasure chest (a Styrofoam ice chest works well) with lots of fun loot (cheap items from the dollar store will do the trick). Bury your treasure chest, then create a map leading the little ones to it. If you have time, dip your map in cooled tea and let it dry crinkled, then burn the edges with a match. Leave the map to the buried treasure someplace where little ones can easily discover it. Grab shovels and flashlights (so cool to do at night) and let the treasure hunt begin.

Ages: 3 and up   *Time:* A couple of hours

What to Do When the Temperatures Plunge

MAKE SNOW CONES

Shave or crush ice in a blender. To make syrup, mix one cup of water with one package of unsweetened Kool-Aid over medium heat. Bring to a boil, then stir in two cups of sugar until dissolved. Allow to cool and thicken. Pour over cones.

Ages: Any   *Time:* 10 minutes

CROSS-COUNTRY SKI

Rent some skis and hit the local golf course.

Ages: Any   *Time:* Varies

PULL YOUR LITTLE ONE TO PRESCHOOL IN A SLED

A great way to get to school! Tell the kids they are on a dogsled. Mush! You could also pretend they're on a magic carpet ride.

Ages: 1–5   *Time:* Minutes

PICK A BOUQUET OF ICICLES

For your favorite ice queens and kings.

Ages: 3–8   *Time:* Minutes

DRIZZLE MAPLE SYRUP ON SNOW

So sweet to take a page out of one of my favorite books growing up—*Little House in the Big Woods* by Laura Ingalls Wilder—and make maple candy! Simply heat maple syrup on the stove, add a bit of vanilla extract, then when it's good and hot pour it onto a plate of clean, fresh snow.

Ages: Any   *Time:* 15–20 minutes

BUILD A SNOW FORT

Wait for a packing-snow day—much better than a powder-snow day. Build bricks with plastic shoe boxes, sand buckets, anything with a fun shape that is easy to fill. Build the perimeter of your fort, spacing the snow bricks a bit apart, then add a top layer with snow bricks straddling the bottom bricks beneath it. Make sure the walls are perpendicular. Add snow between the spaces. Smooth the walls with a shovel. Then dump water on the walls from top to bottom to give it an icy finish.

Ages: 3–8   *Time:* Till they freeze!

☞ **Take Note!**

Warm a wintry day for toddlers with the classic story *The Snowy Day* by Ezra Jack Keats, winner of the 1963 Caldecott Medal. No book better captures the magical excitement of the first snowfall.

PAINT SNOW

Make paintings in the snow with food coloring and a spray bottle.

Ages: 1–4   *Time:* Minutes

MAKE A SNOW GLOBE

Get in the spirit of winter any time of the year, or recap a fun day spent in the snow by making a snow globe with your little ones. Just hot- or superglue a small toy like a snowman to the inside of a baby food jar lid, then fill the jar with water, adding about a teaspoon of glycerin and glitter for fake snow. Glue lid shut and shake! Makes a great holiday decoration too.

Ages: 3–8   *Time:* 30 minutes

▼▼▼▼▼▼▼▼▼▼▼▼▼▼▼▼▼▼▼▼▼▼▼▼▼▼▼▼▼▼▼▼▼

Fun from the Field

If you're reluctant to bundle the kids up and haul them over the river and through the woods for snow fun, try your own run closer to home. Mary W. used to make her own little snow run down her back porch stairs when her kids were little guys by packing snow and icing it down a bit. She'd invite her friends to bring their little ones. It was just enough slope for wee ones without all the hassle of packing up for a sled-riding day across town.

▲▲▲▲▲▲▲▲▲▲▲▲▲▲▲▲▲▲▲▲▲▲▲▲▲▲▲▲▲▲▲▲▲

CHAPTER SEVENTEEN

Memorable Fun

God gave us the gift of life; it is up to us to give ourselves the gift of living well.

—Voltaire

One Big Night of Fun

MUSEUM OVERNIGHTS

If you haven't stayed overnight with the little ones at a great museum, pack your sleeping bags—this is one family adventure you don't want to miss.

You can learn a lot more at the museum at night, since there are fewer people and a lot more time to explore. It's exciting and very hands-on. You'll discover lots of activities you won't find during the day. You might get the chance to hold a tarantula and a hissing cockroach and go behind the scenes with a scientist. There are no crowds to fight, and there's no reason to rush. At times, you truly feel you have the whole museum to yourself. Curl up next to a T. rex, sleep next to the fish, fall asleep under the stars, or come nose to nose with a 727. Little dreams will be rich that night.

Ages: 2–8   *Time:* Overnight

DRIVE-IN MOVIES

Remember the drive-in? Quaint, old-fashioned fun you've probably forgotten. Scope out one in your area and take the kids. If you don't have one close by, hunt for one when your family is on vacation. And don't forget the grocery bags full of popcorn and the bug spray!

Ages: 4 and up   *Time:* One fun evening

☞ **Take Note!**

Your junior high reader may find a nice connection in the coming-of-age novel *The Outsiders* by S. E. Hinton.

BALLROOM DANCING

Enroll the family in a ballroom-dancing or even a square-dancing class.

Ages: 8 and up   *Time:* An afternoon or evening

GO ON A NIGHT HIKE THROUGH THE FOREST

Nothing is more exciting and electrifying—light up your senses with a night hike. Map out your hike in advance, if you can find a spot where (safe) nocturnal creatures roam. Arm your crew with flashlights, forehead lights, glow-in-the-dark garb, and maybe even night-vision goggles. Hike into the darkness, letting the snap and crack of branches underfoot giggly-tingle your senses.

Ages: 3 and up   *Time:* 1 hour

MATCHING MOVIE NIGHT

Fun to do with another family: plan an evening out with the kids, sort of. This is great for the preteen crowd—kids old enough to be on their own, but not too old. Have dinner together with another family—the kids get their own table at the restaurant. Then time two movies, one for the adults and one for the kids. Parents and kids split for the main feature. A great way to get out with couples and with the kids and let the not-so-little ones feel like they had their own night out on the town.

Ages: 10–15   *Time:* A couple of hours

One Year of Fun

MAKE A FAMILY CALENDAR

Each month, work on the photo for next year's calendar, whether it's a leaf-peeping hike in September, everyone in costume in October, or a family snow fight in January.

Ages: 8–12   *Time:* 1 year

TIME-LAPSE PHOTO FUN

Take a picture every day in the same spot—whether as a family or just one person—and edit all the pictures together in a video. It's amazing to watch, especially with little ones, who change so quickly.

Ages: All   *Time:* 1 year

CREATE A MEMORY JAR

Starting on January 1, each day write down at least one good thing that's happened to you—a surprise gift, an accomplished goal, a fun memory—onto a piece of paper, fold, and put in a jar. Then, on December 31, open the jar and read your year of amazing memories.

Ages: 5 and up   *Time:* 1 year

CHAPTER EIGHTEEN

An Entire Day of Fun

All grown-ups were once children, although few of them remember it.

—ANTOINE DE SAINT-EXUPÉRY,
THE LITTLE PRINCE

What if you had one magical day to make everything you do together more fun? An entire day of fun? What would you do? Here are some ideas for one perfect fun family day.

GETTING READY IN THE MORNING

Good fun makes for a great morning, and it's easy to do with a couple of twists in your morning routine. Crank up the tunes for a softer wake-up call, or go silly with an alarm clock that cackles like farm animals. Then, on to a quick bubble bath (why not?) to start the day off with some clean fun. Don't forget the bubble machine! "Splish Splash" could be your tune of choice. For breakfast, surprise them with a breakfast bar, laying out all the foods they can choose from (makes little ones feel like they are at a restaurant). Top off with breakfast smoothies—they taste like milk shakes and only you know they are stuffed with nutritious foods like kale, apples, Greek yogurt, avocado, and whey protein. If a green smoothie makes them turn a little green, put it in a colorful to-go cup with a lid to hide it. Or add beet juice to make everything perfectly pink.

While the kids are munching (or sipping) on breakfast, have them decorate their own lunch bags with wiggle eyes, glitter, and stickers.

Whether you drive or walk together, pick a new path to school. Walkers might even decide to make breakfast a quick picnic that morning. Try walking (or running) backward part of the way. Or invite a special guest star to join you that day— say, a favorite neighbor, Grandma, or a special friend who lives across town.

AFTER SCHOOL

Pick up and take off with a fantastic flight plan of fun. Challenge the little ones to airplane themselves to the car (zoooom!), and you are ready to start your chock-full afternoon of fun. Have a shark-attack snack pack at the ready. Simply cut the top of a gray gift bag (or brown paper bag painted gray) in the shape of a shark's mouth, adding small white triangles cut from paper as teeth and two wiggle eyes. Fill the bag with fun, nutritious foods (sharks need to stay big and strong) and include a fishing line of worms—gummy worms, that is. Easy to do if you punch a hole at the end of a straw with a hole punch. Tie a piece of string through the hole, securing a gummy worm on the end with a colored paper clip that you bend into a hook. Then make the kids feel famous by cranking up songs with the kids' names in them (easy to find with an iTunes search). Then you are off on a mini field trip.

There are many quick stops you can make—like a trip to a nature center, a hike, a local farm to see the cows, a close-by museum, a matinee at an IMAX theater, or a scavenger hunt through the mall where you challenge the kids to find things on a list you put together beforehand. Or simply go to the local pet store together. Pet the puppies. Check out the iguanas. Give all the bunny rabbits funny names.

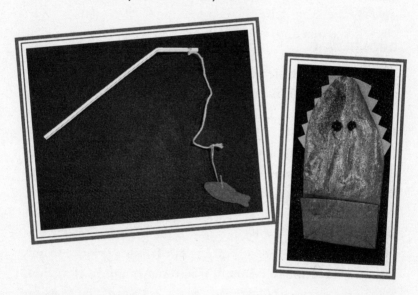

HOMEWORK TIME

Set the thinking mood with classical music, and make some thinking caps to help them get started. To make a thinking cap, roll and staple a square piece of cardboard into a tall, pointy cone; glue on tassels, dots, sparkles, and pom-poms; and stick on jewels or lightning bolts you cut out of bright yellow (or even glow-in-the-dark) poster board to encourage brainstorms. If a snack is in order, bob for apples or sip alphabet soup from a thermos. Tell 'em it's brain food. For pesky questions, set up a Homework Hotline, equipping the kids with walkie-talkies—such a fantastically fun way to ask Mom or Dad math or spelling questions from across the room. Also, give pencil pushing a prod with big fun pencils or personalized pencils, or make fuzzy tops on regular pencils by gluing a bit of craft fur around a pencil top and adding two wiggle eyes.

DINNERTIME

There are a variety of ways you can step up supper; here are a few ideas for inspiration.

Junior Chef Night

Declare it Junior Chef Night, inviting the kids to make dinner. Make it super fun with mini chef hats and aprons the kids decorate with paint pens.

Tailgate Dinner

During football season make your family's favorite team's signature treats, like Primanti's sandwiches for Steelers fans. Set dinner up as a tailgate that night, with artificial grass on the island or the dinner table. Spray-paint field lines on it beforehand. And an electric grill makes hot dog roasting fun. Even turn down the heat and have everyone eat dinner wearing coats, hats, and mittens.

Dinner on the Front Porch

Instead of setting the table, set the front porch one night. Grab your not-so-finest tablecloth and add a vase of flowers or candlesticks for an extra touch.

Make Your Own Pizza

Who doesn't love pizza? Let creative spirits fly and add some fun to dinner with a Make Your Own Pizza night.

THINGS TO ADD FOR EXTRA FUN

Funny Hats

We all wear different hats during the day—brother, son, student, football player—so why not cap the day off with one, letting the kids pick and wear a funny hat to dinner?

A Talking Stick

Make a fun talking stick by wrapping a plain stick with pipe cleaner or adding feathers, and pass it around at dinnertime. Whoever has the talking stick has the floor when it comes to dinner conversation that night. A fun and simple way to encourage kids to speak up at dinnertime.

> **! FUN FACT:**
>
> According to the National Center on Addiction and Substance Abuse (CASA) at Columbia University, families who practice good communication, whether in the car or around the dinner table, are more likely to have children who are substance-free.

BEDTIME FUN

End your day with a fun good-night video you make with the kids. Have them rewrite lyrics to a good-night song— "Good Night, Ladies," "Rock-a-Bye Baby," "Silent Night," or "Sweet Dreams" by Eurythmics. Come up with a simple pj's dance and record it on your phone music-video style. Make it a tribute, a good-night greeting to a faraway relative like grandparents, a traveling dad, or a special aunt, and send. If you give them a bedtime snack, let them make fruit and vegetable puppets. Just pierce an orange with a chopstick, add half a lemon for a hat by poking it with a toothpick, and put a grape on top for a pom-pom. Halved grapes make fun eyes. Cauliflower makes great hair. Use sliced bananas for ears. Get creative, and most of all have FUN!

End the day of fun with a blank storybook. Staple blank pieces of paper together on one side beforehand and hand your child a blank storybook to read to *you* as a good-night story—a blank slate from which to start dreaming and making up all the bedtime story their little mind can muster. Sit and enjoy your time together until their words start to drift off to dreamland . . .

Always kiss your children goodnight, even if they're already asleep.

—H. JACKSON BROWN JR.

Epilogue
What the Fun?!

We are all in this together! I am so happy to spend my days sharing ideas of how to sneak lots of family fun into bits of days. I think we moms and dads get smarter by comparing notes on how we play this important little game called family!

I would love to hear from you about what you do with your family—whether it's ideas and inspirations from the book or just some stuff you cooked up on your own. Let me know at www.DonnaBozzo.com. Can't wait to hear from you! Family fun on!

ACKNOWLEDGMENTS

A world of thanks to my agent, Stacey Glick, and her team at Dystel & Goderich for helping me turn scribbles of ideas into *finally*—ta-da—a book. I cannot tell you how much I appreciate all your hard work. Thank you, Jane Dystel and Jim McCarthy, for originally bringing me into the Dystel fold. And kudos and love to Samantha, Alea, Chelsea, and Talia—my perfect *Today* show assistants—especially Chelsea for powering through because you knew it was live TV.

Thank you to my wonderful editor, Becky Cole. We share a heart when it comes to family and fun. You made this book sing and dance and hula and tango and tango again. Without you, it'd be too messy to read. Thank you. Thank you. Thank you.

To Hoda, Kathie Lee, and Joanne LaMarca and team—such a hoot to play with my gals and let the country have fun along with us.

Of course, I can't do anything without the love of my immediate family; we're so lucky to be together all our days.

Thank you, Matt, Juliana, Grace, and Ava Francesca, for over-looking dishes in the sink and lost permission slips so I could share our family secrets for all to play. I love you all that there is. More than there is.

Thank you to my earliest play group—my cousins Liz, Janice, and Bill, and my sister, Jen. I'll never forget all the house-made fun we had together with our mothers. Thanks to Grandma for your bookshelf of borrow-forever books, and to my cousins-in-law Amy, Megan, and Molly for cheering me on before anyone else. Thank you to my friend Tessa. Who houses a live rooster for me in the name of fun? You do! And so much more for *our* four boys and three girls.

Thanks to my godson Max, his sister Sophie, and their mom for happily following me, video camera in hand, to all ends of the country, from West Virginia to (*where are we??*) Wyoming—all in the name of fun (and research). And to my twenty nieces and nephews who tried out that first alligator bag in Grandma's basement on projects that sometimes took weeks to dry. We never ran out of ways to use up those wiggle eyes.

Thank you to my first-grade teacher, the late Sandy Parker, and all the teachers at Protsman Elementary School for *Hansel and Gretel* plays and sock monkey puppet shows. Each and every time you brought fun into our classroom, it was magic. And to my Protsman playmates for giggly walks home from school, afternoons at Northgate Park, playground football games, and—especially now—silly, silly jump-rope songs. Without one another, we wouldn't be who we are today. In my mind, we still play together every day.

Most of all, thank you to each and every grown-up who stopped the busy world even for a little while to have fun with me. *That* means the world—still, today.

ACKNOWLEDGMENTS

A world of thanks to my agent, Stacey Glick, and her team at Dystel & Goderich for helping me turn scribbles of ideas into *finally*—ta-da—a book. I cannot tell you how much I appreciate all your hard work. Thank you, Jane Dystel and Jim McCarthy, for originally bringing me into the Dystel fold. And kudos and love to Samantha, Alea, Chelsea, and Talia—my perfect *Today* show assistants—especially Chelsea for powering through because you knew it was live TV.

Thank you to my wonderful editor, Becky Cole. We share a heart when it comes to family and fun. You made this book sing and dance and hula and tango and tango again. Without you, it'd be too messy to read. Thank you. Thank you. Thank you.

To Hoda, Kathie Lee, and Joanne LaMarca and team—such a hoot to play with my gals and let the country have fun along with us.

Of course, I can't do anything without the love of my immediate family; we're so lucky to be together all our days.